fanciful felties

from mummysam

Sew People to Meet,
Places to Go & Things to Do

Samantha Cotterill

stashBOOKS

an imprint of C&T Publishing

PUBLISHER: Amy Marson

CREATIVE DIRECTOR: Gailen Runge

ACQUISITIONS EDITOR: Susanne Woods

EDITOR: Lynn Koolish

TECHNICAL EDITOR: Carolyn Aune

COPYEDITOR/PROOFREADER: Wordfirm Inc.

COVER/BOOK DESIGNER: Kristy Zacharias

PAGE LAYOUT ARTIST: Casey Dukes

PRODUCTION COORDINATOR: Zinnia Heinzmann

PRODUCTION EDITOR: Julia Cianci

ILLUSTRATOR: Samantha Cotterill

PHOTOGRAPHY BY Christina Carty-Francis and Diane Pedersen of C&T Publishing, Inc., unless otherwise noted

Published by Stash Books, an imprint of C&T Publishing, Inc., P.O. Box 1456, Lafayette, CA 94549

Library of Congress Cataloging-in-Publication Data

Cotterill, Samantha.

Fanciful felties from mummysam : sew people to meet, places to go & things to do / Samantha Cotterill.

   p. cm.

ISBN 978-1-60705-006-3 (softcover)

1. Felt work. 2. Soft sculpture. I. Title.

TT849.5.C685 2010

746'.0463--dc22

2009053523

Printed in China

10 9 8 7 6 5 4 3 2 1

ACKNOWLEDGMENTS

Many, many thanks to:

Etsy—the online marketplace for artisans that led C&T's acquisitions editor to discover my work and for giving me this wonderful opportunity to write a book.

My acquisitions editor, Susanne Woods—besides our connection through fruit pastilles, she was the one who approached me in the first place and believed I could create a great book.

Lynn Koolish—a wonderful editor who helped a first-time writer create something very special.

My two cheeky little monkeys—although not every color suggestion from enthusiastic six- and three-year-olds was taken, every word of encouragement ("you're the awesomest maker, Mum") helped inspire this mummy to believe she could do it.

My fantastic husband, Lucious—his never-ending support and midnight latte deliveries were crucial to getting through some very late nights. I still can't believe he encouraged me to continue sewing after seeing my first attempt at a felt cupcake. Oh my, how dreadful it was.

My mum, dad, and sister—their individual talents kept steering me in the right direction. (You really can't go wrong when you have two writers and an amazing artist in the family.)

My amazing babysitter Sam—without her complete flexibility to come whenever I needed her, this book may never have been finished. Seriously.

My Canadian soulmates Darcy and Nicole—they have believed in me since the first day I sputtered out a respectable "eh?"

The entire C&T staff—their dedication and hard work helped take this project from piles of doodles and notes to a beautiful piece of art.

contents

RON
RON

ron
SEW
SEW
SEW

on

sew

PIN
PIN

PIN
SEW

on

SEW

pin

sew

PIN

SEW

Pin

v

SEW

pin

sew

PIN

y

SEW

PIN

Sew

PIN

SEW PIN

sew

pin

SEW

PIN

sew

PIN

SEW

pin

SEW

PIN

SEW

PIN

T
TR

trace

TRA
trace

tra

trace

TRACE

trace

TRACE

trace

TRACE

FOREWORD

by Julie Schneider, Etsy.com

I've loved Samantha Cotterill's work—with its meandering lines, endearing characters, and quirky scenarios that she brings to life from her needle, thread, and pen—since the moment I first stumbled into her world through the garden gate of her Etsy shop, mummysam. In my daily explorations of the craft world, whether I'm traipsing around Etsy online at work, or out at a bustling gallery opening, I thrive on staying up-to-date on the current makings and movements in the handmade universe. There are certain special artists whose work I encounter that immediately finds it way into a distinctly shaped empty niche near and dear to my heart, like a puzzle piece I didn't realize I was missing, and sparks something within me to pick up my own pen to start sketching and making something new that perhaps I hadn't been making time for in my life. Sam's work has this pull on me. Luckily for all of us with creative curiosity, Sam's talents have been given their own deserved spotlight in the form of this book, to continue to inspire and encourage this burgeoning gen-eration of makers to play and experiment and follow a sewing needle to discovery.

INTRODUCTION

The projects in this book are simple. The mate-rials used are minimal, and the directions are easy to follow. The complexity lies in what you do with it and where you let it take you. Don't worry if sewing is something new; I dove into this medium head-first, with not so much as a clue as to how to thread a needle. The projects are uncomplicated and can easily be completed in an afternoon. If you are an experienced sewer, then look at this book as a tool to inspire you in your own work.

The projects are designed to encourage experi-mentation. Don't care too much for the shutters on the Country Cottage? Just flip to the back of the book for more shutter ideas, or go off on your own and do something *you* like. Play around with the threads, change the fabrics, and sketch your own ideas. Sew new lines; eliminate others. Take it as far as you can go, and watch as the artist in you emerges.

All of the materials required to complete the projects are readily available—if not at stores, then easily online. Refer to the Resources (page 94) for a complete list of quality suppliers. Scan through The Essentials (pages 6–13) to find out what you will need in order to start, as well as to learn some basics or simply freshen up on some forgotten techniques, including all the stitches needed to complete every project in this book.

I hope this book becomes part of your perma-nent collection, a book to pick up when starting to sew, a book to revisit when feeling stuck in your own work, and a book to just look pretty when it's sitting on the shelf—the more dog-eared the pages, the better!

the essentials

GETTING STARTED

Bits and Bobs

You will need the following supplies for the projects in this book.
(Read on for more information about each item in the list.)

- Wool felt
- Selection of cotton fabrics
- Embroidery floss
- Assorted hand-sewing and embroidery needles
- Assorted machine threads
- Stuffing

- Paper-backed fusible web
- Fabric stabilizer
- Transfer marker or tool
- Iron
- Scissors
- Seam ripper (if you are anything like me)

- Point turner (The end of a paintbrush or a chopstick is a great alternative.)
- Straight pins
- Sewing machine (Many a project in this book can be created by hand if a machine is not available.)

Natural Fabrics

Coming from a world of painting and drawing, I wanted to create images out of thread. I needed a material sturdy enough to handle the demands of my forever-moving needle without losing its shape. 100% wool felt is amazing to work with and gives you the freedom to explore this idea without needing a stabilizer or a hoop. Wool may be prewashed, but be aware that the wool's smooth texture may give way to a more nubbly appearance. If you want to maintain a smoother texture, just spot clean unwanted marks with warm, soapy water.

Cotton is a natural fiber that makes a wonderful accompaniment for felt. Heavier cottons work quite easily with embroidery, but don't shy away from experimenting with more delicate materials. By using an embroidery hoop or fabric stabilizer, you will have endless possibilities and the potential to take advantage of a whole new set of materials once thought unworkable. (Do grandma's old curtains look more interesting now?) I highly recommend preshrinking your cotton before sewing; putting the fabric through a wash and dry cycle drastically reduces the chance of your embroidered imagery distorting should you have to wash it later.

Embroidery Floss

Skeins of embroidery floss are the most commonly used threads when working with hand embroidery. Packaged in small bundles, each thread comes in six plies and can easily be divided into a smaller number of plies for finer detail.

When using a skein of floss, remove the wrappers, and then wrap the floss around a floss bobbin (a small piece of cardboard designed to hold floss, which can be found at virtually any needlework or craft shop). After jotting down the color identification number (printed on the floss wrapper) on the back of the bobbin, simply place it in a container designed to hold bobbins. Yes, Mum, I know; I should listen to my own advice. Staring at a pile of knotted thread permanently tangled with other knotted thread while writing this important notation does not reflect well on me.

Needles

Your first trip to the fabric store may be quite overwhelming, but don't let it be. Upon seeing a wall filled with an endless array of needles in varying shapes and sizes, the task of picking the "right" one can seem daunting. Don't panic. The best thing to do in such a situation is to purchase a variety packet of needles and go from there. As long as the needle end is sharp, the eye large enough to accommodate embroidery floss, and the length of the needle somewhere in the middle, then all is good. Large-eyed needles are lovely to work with when using all six plies of embroidery floss, whereas small-eyed needles are perfect for sewing thread or just a few strands of floss.

Stuffing

You have numerous possibilities when it comes to stuffing your pieces. Experiment until you find something suitable for your needs. Pure wool stuffing is a lovely material that not only stuffs beautifully but is also completely natural and thus perfect when making things for children. You may find polyester fiberfill more to your liking, or you might branch out even further and try old fabric scraps, rice, beans, or crushed walnut shells. Use this time to find out how each material affects the way your pieces sit. Pretty soon you will find a combination that suits you perfectly.

Scissors

Sharp, tiny scissors are absolutely essential for embroidering and working with felt. Not only are they handy for quickly snipping off leftover floss, they are also great for cutting out ridiculously small shapes of felt. But please be careful—I have made many an overly confident "snip" that has caused unwanted fabric to get cut as well. Drats.

Transfer Tools

Saral Wax-Free Transfer Paper
Saral Transfer Paper is a great way to transfer designs onto felt. If you choose a paper in a contrasting color, the transferred design will be easy to read on either light- or dark-colored felt. Saral paper is readily available at art supply stores and some fabric/craft stores.

Tracing Paper or Golden Threads Paper
These transparent papers make it easy to trace the design, and because they are so lightweight, they can be sewn right through.

Gluestick
Use a light touch of gluestick to hold tracing or Golden Threads paper in place when stitching.

Silicone ART Paper
Silicone ART Paper (from C&T Publishing) is designed for use with fusible appliqué but can also be used for transferring images. Photocopy a design onto the ART paper using a laser printer, and simply iron the design onto the felt.

Fabric Stabilizers

When you are ready to explore embroidering on fabric other than sturdy wool felt, fabric stabilizers will come in handy. Fabric stabilizers provide a more solid base to work on, ensuring that your stitched image remains beautifully intact, without buckling and puckering. Cut out a piece of stabilizer slightly larger than your design, and apply it to the back side of the fabric. Once your design is embroidered, remove the stabilizer, stand back, and admire what you have just accomplished. Many different types of stabilizers are available, so take some time to experiment with different products until you find one that most suits your working style.

THE TECHNIQUES

Transferring a Design

Saral Wax-Free Transfer Paper
Place your felt on a hard surface with the pattern on top. Slide a piece of Saral paper (colored side down) between the two layers, and proceed to trace over the design with a blunt tool (dry ballpoint pens, pencils, and knitting needles are all great options). When you are stitching, be careful that you don't rub your hand over the lines as you work; otherwise, the chalk marks may begin to fade. If this does happen, simply go back over the lines with a chalk pencil.

Tracing Paper
Use tracing paper (or a paper designed specifically for this purpose, such as Golden Threads), and trace the design using a fairly light pencil. Pin or use a gluestick to lightly glue the paper to the felt, and stitch through the paper. Once you have finished stitching the design, tear away the paper and remove any remaining tiny pieces with a pair of tweezers. Spritzing the paper with water may help in removal.

Silicone ART Paper

Photocopy the design onto the Silicone ART Paper using a laser printer. (If you do not own a laser printer, copy shops use laser printers.) Place the ART paper face down on the felt and iron to transfer the design. Stitch the design. The transferred image is permanent, but it is light and the excess laser toner can be brushed off the felt. Your images will be the reverse of the original but this may not matter. Your characters will just face the opposite direction. If you want your softies to face in the same direction as those in the book, make a photocopy of the design from the book. Using a lightbox or window, trace the photocopied image onto the back of the paper. Copy your newly traced image onto the release paper. Make sure to check your copier's functions first, as many can easily reverse the image for you.

Take the time to explore what this paper can do for you. If you are using pure wool felt, you may find the image more faded than if a synthetic blend is used. Once you have found a fabric that lends itself really well to this method, you can embroider your design with no worry of markings disappearing as you work.

Handling Curves

Just a few properly placed snips will make it much easier to turn pieces right side out. The smooth edges that result from taking a little extra time to clip around tight corners also help you get a more finished look. (Oh my, you should see my first 100 dolls before I learned that trick.)

There are basically two types of curves: concave and convex. The techniques needed to approach each one are slightly different.

Clipping is used for concave curves, or when the cut edge is shorter than the stitching line. By making a series of small snips in the seam allowance, you allow the piece to lie flat once turned or pressed (see Figure 1). Make sure your cuts stay safely out of the stitching; otherwise, defeat will set in when your finger pokes through a big hole in your beloved piece.

Notching is needed when the cut edge of a convex curve is longer than the stitching line. This process involves cutting a series of small triangles from the seam allowance to remove the extra fabric, which would otherwise create very bulky folds (see Figure 2).

Pinking shears are good tools to use when you want to do a series of quick notches; just cut along the edge of the fabric.

Figure 1

Figure 2

Stitching

Although I do all of my pieces by machine, there is no rule saying that you have to. In fact, this book has been designed to make it easy for those of you who would rather tackle the projects by hand, or you can mix hand and machine stitching. If you are not interested in working by hand, then simply go over the transferred lines with a machine instead.

MACHINE STITCHING

Even when working with a machine, you can achieve a more drawn look with your stitching. Simply follow these steps to have more creative control with your machine:

For complete control of your machine stitching, disengage or cover the feed dogs. Do this either by lowering them or using a cover plate (refer to your sewing machine manual as needed). Either way, the fabric will no longer automatically feed through the machine, which means you must do all the maneuvering.

Set the stitch width and length to zero, and give yourself ample time to practice and experiment. This technique takes a bit of getting used to, so practice on fabric that you don't care too much about. All the projects in the book involve felt, which is sturdy enough for this approach without using a hoop for support. Just make sure to hold the felt taut as you move it around. (I tend to lick my fingers periodically throughout the process. It allows them to stick to the fabric a bit better, thus giving me a better handle on the material when stitching the lines.)

Take this opportunity to sew completely freehand (free-motion), using the pattern only as a guide. Trying to make everything look perfect will make the project look stilted and won't allow your own natural tendencies to come out. A crooked line here and there won't hurt—it will give the project character and make it *yours*.

HAND STITCHING

By learning just a few stitches, you will be ready to take off and master all the projects in this book. Once you are comfortable with the following stitches, try adding even more to your library. Then start playing to see how to combine various stitches to create something entirely your own.

Straight or Running Stitch

What a simple and wonderful way to ease yourself into embroidery. Bring your needle up through the back of the fabric at A and down again through B. It's as simple as that. Repeat this step at regular intervals to create a straight running stitch (Figure 3). This stitch gives a broken-line appearance and can easily be worked to create straight or curved lines.

Seeding or seed stitching (Figure 4) is the art of placing straight stitches in a random pattern throughout your working area.

Split Stitch

If you are anything like me, you will get absolutely hooked on the split stitch. This stitch produces such beautiful thick lines and lends itself not only to straight lines but to delicious, curvy ones as well.

Starting in the same manner as the straight stitch, bring your needle up through the back of your fabric at A and down again through B (Figure 5). Now bring your needle back up halfway through your completed stitch at C (Figure 6), splitting the thread in half. Repeat this cycle of stitching and splitting until you have reached the desired length (Figure 7).

Back Stitch

This wonderful stitch enables you to achieve a very clean and solid outline. In the back stitch, you work the needle in the *opposite* direction of your working line. Bring the needle up through the back of your fabric at A, and move in the opposite direction down through B (Figure 8). Then bring the needle out ahead of A at C. Repeat by bringing the needle down again at A and out ahead of C.

Figure 3 | *Straight or Running Stitch*

Figure 4 | *Seeding or Seed Stitching*

Figure 5 | *Split Stitch*   **Figure 6**

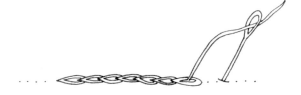

Figure 7

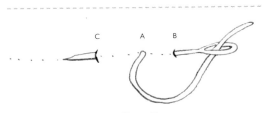

Figure 8

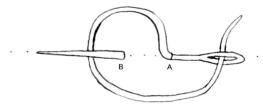

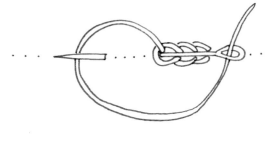

Figure 9 | *Chain Stitch*

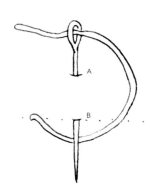

Figure 10

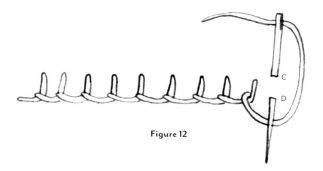

Figure 11 | *Blanket Stitch*

Chain Stitch

One of my favorite stitches (it makes smashing sweater patterns for dolls) is the chain stitch, which creates a line that is slightly more raised. To make things simpler, try working on the stitch from top to bottom. Bring the needle up through A, and go back down through the same hole, making sure to leave a loop (see Figure 9). Bring the needle back up at B and through the loop on your stitching line. Repeat the entire process until you have reached the desired length (Figure 10). Finally, simply secure the last loop with a vertical stitch over the end of the remaining loop.

Blanket Stitch

The versatile blanket stitch is quite lovely for edgings, borders, and appliqué. In this book, the blanket stitch is used mainly as a beautiful way to close up many of the projects. Push the needle down through A and up on the stitching line at B (Figure 11). Push the needle back down at C and up again at D, making sure the needle is over the loop (Figure 12). Pull the thread tight, and repeat the entire process. Then simply secure the last loop with a small stitch.

Cross Stitch

One of the only stitches where your threads actually cross over each other, this stitch adds great decorative detail to your work. Create these X's by bringing your needle up in a diagonal line from A to B (Figure 13). Then continue your stitch from C to D. For a neater look, try making sure all the top threads in the X's are going in the same direction.

Figure 12

French Knot

A single French knot can be used to make a delicate little dot, or many can be scattered about to add texture to a larger area. Bring the needle up through A. While holding the thread taut between your fingers, wrap the thread around the base of your needle twice (Figure 14). Continue to hold the thread taut as you insert the needle back through B, making sure to keep the thread close to the fabric as you go through (Figure 15).

Satin Stitch

Filling an area with straight lines is a quick way to smoothly fill in small areas. Although the satin stitch appears to be one of the easier ones to master, don't panic when you find your first few attempts looking a bit off. It takes a while to get the feel of this stitch, and it may take several more attempts until you get the hang of it. Bring the needle up through A on one side of your design and back down through B on the other side (you may find better results keeping the stitches in a diagonal direction). Work the next stitch close to the first one, going in the same direction as before (Figure 16).

Whip Stitch

A whip stitch, which is great for decoratively joining two pieces of fabric, is one of the easiest stitches to learn. Starting from either the back side of the fabric or in between the two fabric pieces, bring your needle up through A. Pass over the fabric edge with your needle, and bring it back through at B (Figure 17). Continue working along the edges of the fabrics, trying to keep your strokes even lengthwise and an equal distance apart.

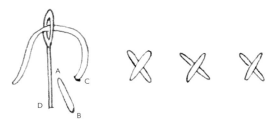

Figure 13 | *Cross Stitch*

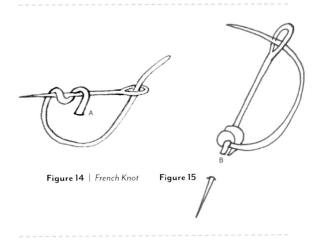

Figure 14 | *French Knot*   **Figure 15**

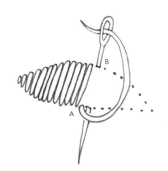

Figure 16 | *Satin Stitch*

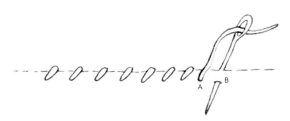

Figure 17 | *Whip Stitch*

uptown

charles

FINISHED SIZE: 3˝W × 7˝H × 2˝D

Dressed for a night out, Charles is ready to hop on the double-decker bus and head into the city. Mix and match his vest and jacket, or try substituting a patterned fabric for his vest. He is fun to customize and makes a perfect gift for those city dwellers in your life.

Materials

White wool felt: 4˝ × 6˝

Cool blue wool felt: 3˝ × 3½˝

Charcoal gray wool felt: 5˝ × 6˝

Scrap of wool felt
for the base: 3˝ × 3˝

Scrap of brown wool felt
for the mustache

Patterned cotton
for the back: 5˝ × 9˝

Charcoal gray and light gray
embroidery floss

Stuffing (page 7)

*The author used Holland Wool
felt in Soft White, Cool Blue,
Charcoal, and Coffee (see
Resources, page 94).*

Stitches

Back stitch (page 11)

Straight stitch (page 11)

Blanket stitch (page 12)

Instructions

Patterns are on pages 68–69.

1. Use your preferred method (pages 8–9) to transfer Charles's face and torso to the white felt. Embroider the design. Do not cut out the face. (Figure 1)

2. Cut out the vest from the cool blue felt. Transfer the design onto the vest; embroider. Pin the vest in place on Charles's head and face. Use dark gray thread to stitch the vest to the body along the vest's top neckline. (Figure 2)

3. Transfer the jacket design onto the charcoal gray felt, and embroider with the light gray floss. Cut out the jacket along the dashed line, and pin it in place on top of the vest, using the pattern as a guide. Attach the jacket to the vest by stitching along the top edge of the jacket. (Figure 3)

4. Place Charles on the cotton fabric, right sides together, making sure to extend the cotton ½˝ beyond the bottom of the felt piece. Sew Charles to the cotton, ⅛˝ outside the design's edge. Leave the bottom section open. Trim any extra fabric from the sides and top, and clip the curved seams (page 9). (Figure 4)

5. Turn Charles right side out, and fold the bottom cotton edge into the body. Stuff. (Figure 5)

6. Stand Charles on top of the felt for the base, and trace around the base (Figure 6). Cut out the felt, and attach it using a blanket stitch in dark gray embroidery floss.

7. Cut out the mustache from a scrap of dark brown felt, and attach it to the face with a couple of stitches at the center. (Figure 7)

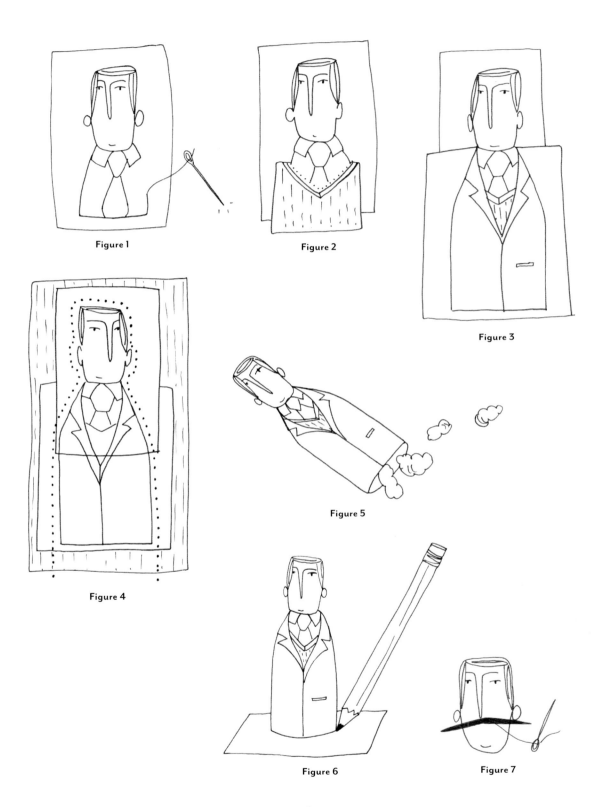

Figure 1

Figure 2

Figure 3

Figure 4

Figure 5

Figure 6

Figure 7

marge

FINISHED SIZE: 3½˝W × 11˝H × 3˝D

My own Marge sits adoringly on my fireplace, as she is one of my favorite possessions. Marge began my love for sewing people, and I am always looking for ways to reinvent her. It's the tiny changes that can take a project to the next level. Shorten the jacket, and Marge has gone from attending the opera to joining some good friends out for lunch. (Albeit a nice luncheon, don't you think?)

Materials

White wool felt: 4˝ × 7˝

Warm gray wool felt: 6˝ × 7½˝

Yellow ochre wool felt: 2˝ × 12˝

Scrap of wool felt
for the base: 4˝ × 4˝

Patterned cotton: 1 piece 5˝ × 7˝
for the skirt, 1 piece 6˝ × 13˝
for the back

Charcoal gray, orange, yellow,
and cream embroidery floss

Stuffing (page 7)

*The author used Holland Wool felt in
Soft White, Cocoa, and Ochre (see
Resources, page 94).*

Stitches

Straight stitch (page 11)

Split stitch (page 11)

Back stitch (page 11)

Blanket stitch (page 12)

Instructions

Patterns are on pages 70–71.

1. Use your preferred method (pages 8–9) to transfer Marge's face and torso to the white felt. Embroider the design, but do not cut it out yet. (Figure 1)

2. Cut out the front skirt fabric. Using the pattern as a guide, place the embroidered face/torso upside down on the fabric, right sides together. Join the pieces by stitching across the top, using a ¼˝ seam. (Figure 2)

Figure 1

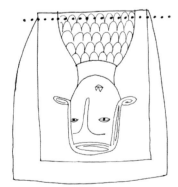

Figure 2

3. Unfold the sewn piece, and press flat with a warm iron.

4. Place Marge on the remaining cotton fabric, right sides together. Sew the body to the cotton, keeping a ⅛″ distance outside the edge of the embroidered design and using a ¼″ seam allowance once you hit the skirt. Leave the bottom section open. (Figure 3)

5. Trim any extra fabric from the sides and top, and clip the curved seams (page 9). Turn Marge right side out, turn the bottom cotton edge into the body, and stuff. (Figure 4)

6. Use the warm gray felt rectangle for the jacket. Blanket stitch around the entire perimeter using three-ply cream embroidery floss. Set aside.

7. Cut a ¼″ × 12″ strip from the yellow ochre felt for the belt. Fold each belt end in half, and make a diagonal cut. Wrap the jacket around Marge, and secure it with the belt by tying a simple knot in the back. Fold over the front corners of the jacket. (Figure 5)

8. Stand Marge on top of the scrap of fabric for the base, and trace around the base (see Figure 6, page 17). Cut out the felt, and attach it using a blanket stitch in orange embroidery floss.

9. To embellish her hair, cut a ¾″ × 6″ strip from the yellow ochre felt. Straight stitch along one edge, using yellow embroidery floss. Pull the thread taut until you have made a circle; then sew the ends together. Attach the embellishment to Marge's hair. (Figure 6)

Figure 3

Figure 4

Figure 5

Figure 6

city car

FINISHED SIZE: 6˝W × 3½˝H × 2˝D

Small and light, this car would make a great gift for any little city dweller. This project is also a great way to familiarize yourself with some free-motion stitching (page 10) if you want to have a go at it. You will never know unless you give it a try!

Materials

Ochre wool felt: 9˝ × 5˝

White wool felt:
1 piece 5˝ × 3˝,
1 piece 5˝ × 2˝

Green wool felt: 5˝ × 2˝

Sea green wool felt: 3˝ × 3˝

Patterned cotton fabric
for the back: 8½˝ × 5˝

Charcoal gray and
light blue embroidery floss

Stuffing (page 7)

*The author used Holland Wool felt in
Ochre, Soft White, Willow, and Sea
Green (see Resources, page 94).*

Stitches

Straight stitch (page 11)

Back stitch (page 11)

Whip stitch (page 13)

Instructions

Patterns are on page 72.

1. Use your preferred method (pages 8–9) to transfer the car outline onto the ochre felt. Embroider the design, but do not cut it out yet. (Figure 1)

2. Transfer the window onto the white felt. Embroider the design. Cut out the window, making sure to leave a ⅛˝ clearance around the outside edge of the design. Position the window on the car according to the pattern, and pin it in place. With a matching sewing thread (or one-ply embroidery floss), stitch around the edge of the window through both layers of felt, using small straight stitches. (Figure 2)

3. Cut out the side panel from the green felt. Pin the appliqué shape in place on top of the ochre felt. Embroider around the inside edge, using charcoal gray embroidery floss and making sure to go through both layers of felt. (Figure 3)

4. Transfer the 2 wheels onto the white felt. Embroider the wheels according to the pattern, and then cut along the dotted lines. Cut out the car, using the pattern as a guide. Pin the wheels in place from underneath the car. With a matching sewing thread (or one-ply embroidery floss), stitch around the edge where the car meets the wheel, using small straight stitches. Cut out the fender pieces from the sea green felt, and pin them in place over each wheel. Use light blue embroidery floss to attach the fender to the car by embroidering small straight stitches around the outside edge of the fender. (Figure 4)

5. Place the car on the cotton fabric, right sides together, making sure to extend the cotton ½˝ beyond the bottom of the felt piece. Sew around the edges, ⅛˝ outside the edge of the design, leaving a 2˝ opening at the bottom. Trim any extra fabric from the sides and top, and clip or notch any curved seams (page 9). Turn the car right side out through the opening; then stuff.

6. Stitch the opening closed using a whip stitch in a matching thread. (Figure 5)

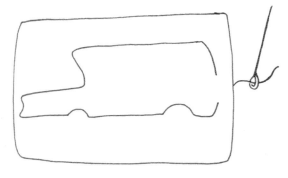

Figure 1

Figure 2

Figure 3

Figure 4

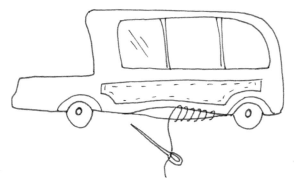

Figure 5

city brownstone

FINISHED SIZE: 3˝W × 12˝H × 2½˝D

This city brownstone has a classic look that will not only last a lifetime of play but will also look stunning when displayed on a shelf. This project is a fun one, especially if you are comfortable using free-motion stitching (page 10). For hand embroidery, it may take some extra patience, but the end result will be so worth the effort.

For fun, flip to pages 92–93, and experiment with different windows and doors. Simply reduce or enlarge the window and door options to your own desired size. With one quick switch, you can take your city brownstone straight from uptown right to the heart of the fashion district.

Materials

White wool felt: 8˝ × 6˝

Light orange wool felt:
6˝ × 10˝

Dark orange wool felt:
1 piece 6˝ × 6˝ for the roof,
1 piece 2˝ × 4˝ for the
door panels

Yellow ochre wool felt:
1 piece 2˝ × 5˝ for the door,
1 piece 4˝ × 2˝ for
the shutters

Scrap of wool felt
for the base: 3˝ × 4˝

Patterned cotton fabric:
1 piece 5˝ × 13˝ for the back,
1 piece 1½˝ × 2½˝
for the chimney back

Charcoal gray, white,
light blue, light orange, and
ochre embroidery floss

Stuffing (page 7)

*The author chose Holland
Wool felt in Soft White,
Apricot, Carrot, and Ochre
(see Resources, page 94).*

Stitches

Straight stitch (page 11)

Back stitch (page 11)

Blanket stitch (page 12)

Instructions

Patterns are on pages 73–74.

1. Cut out the brownstone house shape from the light orange felt.

2. Use your preferred method (pages 8–9) to transfer the roof shingles design onto the dark orange felt. (You may also choose to free-motion stitch this design without following a pattern.) Cut out the roof. Embroider the design.

3. Place the roof upside down and wrong side up on top of the house. Stitch the pieces together along the top edge, using a ¼˝ seam allowance (Figure 1). Unfold the sewn piece, and iron flat.

4. Transfer the windows to the white felt, and embroider the design. Cut along the dashed lines, and pin them in position on the house. Use a matching sewing thread (or one-ply embroidery floss) to stitch around the perimeters of the windows using straight stitches. Make sure to go through both layers of felt (Figure 2). Repeat this step for the door background.

5. Cut out the door from the ochre felt and the door panels from the dark orange felt. Attach the cut panels using a back stitch in charcoal gray around the perimeter of each panel. Make sure to go through both layers of felt. Pin the door in place on top of the door background. Use charcoal gray embroidery floss and a straight stitch to stitch around the perimeter of the door, making sure to go through all layers of felt.

6. Cut out the shutters from the ochre felt. Pin the shutters in place over each window. Embroider the shutters, going through both layers of felt as you sew. (Figure 3)

7. Cut out the window adornments, and position them on the windows. With charcoal gray embroidery thread, attach the adornments to the window, using a small straight stitch around the perimeter. (Figure 4)

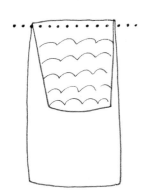

Figure 1

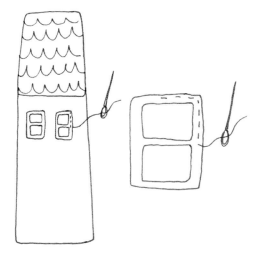

Figure 2

Figure 3

Figure 4

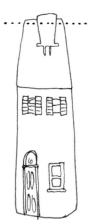

Figure 5

Figure 6

8. Transfer the chimney to the white felt, and embroider the design. Place the chimney on the cotton, right sides together, and sew them together, keeping a ⅛″ distance outside the edge of the design. Leave the bottom section open. Trim away any excess material, and clip or notch any tight curves (page 9). Turn the chimney right side out through the opening, and lightly stuff. Position the chimney upside down and fabric side out when pinning it in place on the cottage roof. (Figure 5)

9. Place the brownstone on the cotton fabric, right sides together, making sure to extend the cotton ½″ beyond the bottom of the felt piece. Sew the brownstone to the fabric, ⅛″ outside the edge of the design. Leave the bottom section open.

10. Trim extra fabric from the sides and top, and cut small notches around any hard corners to allow for a smoother shape. Turn the brownstone right side out, and fold the bottom cotton edge into the house. Stuff. (Figure 6)

11. Stand the brownstone on top of the scrap of felt for the base, and trace around the base (see Figure 6, page 17). Cut out the felt, and attach it with a blanket stitch in light orange embroidery floss.

down country

simon

FINISHED SIZE: 2¼˝W × 5˝H × 1½˝D

Oh, Simon, when are you going to learn? Filling your school bag with toy planes and comics is not going to get you higher grades!

Making Simon was so much fun, but making up a story to go along with him was even more so. Use this project to make up your own story. Change his hair color, and add some French knot freckles. Who knows, you may end up with a Liam instead (and I've heard they don't hide toys in their bags).

Materials

White wool felt: 3½″ × 6½″

Green wool felt: 3½″ × 4½″

Yellow wool felt: ½″ × 7″

Dark brown wool felt
for hair: 2½″ × 2½″

Light brown wool felt
for bag: 5″ × 7″

Scrap of wool felt
for the base: 3″ × 3″

Patterned cotton
for the back: 4″ × 6½″

Charcoal gray, tan,
dark green, lime green, and
cream embroidery floss

Stuffing (page 7)

*The author used Holland Wool
felt in Soft White, Willow,
Yellow, Brown, and Mocha
(see Resources, page 94).*

Stitches

Back stitch (page 11)

Blanket stitch (page 12)

French knot (page 13)

Satin stitch (page 13)

Instructions

Patterns are on page 75.

1. Use your preferred method (pages 8–9) to transfer Simon's face and torso to the white felt. Embroider the design. Do not cut out the face and torso. (Figure 1)

2. Cut out Simon's hair, and pin it in place on his head, using the pattern as a guide. Embroider the hair, making sure to go through both layers of felt. (Figure 2) **Note:** You may choose not to put a jacket on Simon. In that case, go to Step 4.

3. Cut out the jacket from the green felt along the dashed lines. Embroider the crest and the jacket. Pin the jacket on the face and torso piece, and stitch along the top of the jacket to attach. (Figure 2)

Figure 1

Figure 2

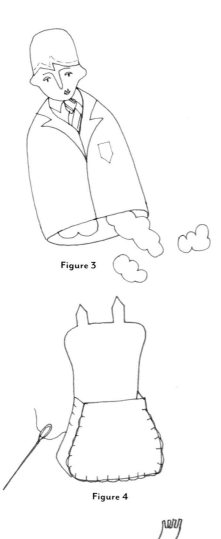

Figure 3

Figure 4

Figure 5

4. Place Simon on the cotton fabric, right sides together, making sure to extend the cotton ½˝ beyond the bottom of the felt piece. Sew Simon to the cotton, ⅛˝ outside the edge of the design. Leave the bottom section open. Trim any extra fabric from the sides and top, and clip the curved seams (page 9).

5. Turn Simon right side out, and fold the bottom cotton edge into the body. Stuff. (Figure 3)

6. Stand Simon on top of the scrap of felt for the base, and trace around the base (see Figure 6, page 17). Cut out the felt, and attach it with a blanket stitch in cream embroidery floss.

7. For Simon's bag, cut out the bag shapes from the light brown felt. Cut the gusset ⅜˝ × 4˝ and the strap ⅜˝ × 5¾˝. Embroider the bag front and back to each side of the gusset, using a blanket stitch in cream embroidery floss (Figure 4). Use a simple cross stitch to attach the strap to each side of the bag. Secure the front straps to the bag with a single French knot on each strap.

8. Use the yellow wool felt for the scarf. Cut small slits in either end of the scarf. Wrap the scarf around Simon's neck to keep him nice and warm! (Figure 5)

Dressed for warmth, Collin is ready to sit by the fire for a good night of cozy reading. Take this opportunity to try some different stitch patterns for his sweater (alternate sweater patterns are on page 76). Or add a jacket—maybe he needs to get out of the house for a bit!

collin

FINISHED SIZE: 3″W × 7″H × 2″D

Materials

White wool felt: 4˝ × 6˝

Yellow ochre wool felt: 4˝ × 6˝

Brown wool felt
for the mustache: ½˝ × 2½˝

Scrap of wool felt
for the base: 3˝ × 3˝

Patterned cotton
for the back: 5˝ × 9˝

Charcoal gray, dark brown,
light blue, and yellow ochre
embroidery floss

Stuffing (page 7)

*The author used Holland Wool felt
in Soft White, Yellow Ochre, and
Coffee (see Resources, page 94).*

Stitches

Split stitch (page 11)

Back stitch (page 11)

Blanket stitch (page 12)

Instructions

Patterns are on pages 75–76.

1. Use your preferred method (pages 8–9) to transfer Collin's face to the white felt. Embroider the design. Do not cut out the face. (Figure 1)

2. Transfer Collin's sweater to the yellow ochre felt, and embroider the design. (Figure 2)

3. Cut out the sweater along the dashed lines. Backstitch the sweater to the face at the neckline, using dark brown thread. (Figure 3)

4. Place Collin on the cotton fabric, right sides together, making sure to extend the cotton ½˝ beyond the bottom of the felt piece. Sew Collin to the cotton, ⅛˝ outside the edge of the design. Leave the bottom section open. Trim any extra fabric from the sides and top, and clip the curved seams (page 9). (Figure 4)

5. Turn Collin right side out, and fold the bottom cotton edge into the body. Stuff. (Figure 5)

6. Stand Collin on top of the scrap of felt for the base, and trace around the base (see Figure 6, page 17). Cut out the felt, and attach it with a blanket stitch in yellow ochre embroidery floss.

7. Cut out the mustache from a scrap of dark brown felt, and attach it to the face with a couple of stitches at the center.

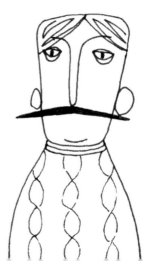

Figure 1

Figure 2

Figure 3

Figure 4

Figure 5

Mr. Bunny looks so studious in his overcoat as he heads to the library to read the morning paper. This is a lovely, simple project that will allow you to make your own little library companion in no time. Once the project is finished, try experimenting with some of the stitches you have learned (pages 11–13) to make him your own. By simply changing the stitching on the sweater, you can create a whole new Mr. Bunny (maybe one who prefers going to the pub instead).

mr. bunny

FINISHED SIZE: 3˝W × 9˝H × 2˝D

Materials

White wool felt: 4˝ × 6˝

Light green wool felt: 5˝ × 7˝

Wool felt of your choice
for sweater stripes: 5˝ × 2˝

Brown wool felt: 3˝ × 7˝

Scrap of wool felt
for the base: 4˝ × 3˝

Patterned cotton
for the back: 5˝ × 11˝

Charcoal gray, brown, and
light green embroidery floss

Stuffing (page 7)

*The author used Holland Wool felt in
colors Soft White, Celery, Willow, and
Coffee (see Resources, page 94).*

Stitches

Straight stitch (page 11)

Blanket stitch (page 12)

Back stitch (page 11)

Satin stitch (page 13)

Instructions

Patterns are on pages 77.

1. Use your preferred method (pages 8–9) to transfer Mr. Bunny's face to the white felt. Embroider the design. (Figure 1)

2. Cut out the shape along the bottom dashed line, leaving the head and ears untrimmed.

3. Cut out Mr. Bunny's body from the light green felt.

4. Using the felt color of your choice, cut 6 strips ¼˝ by approximately 4˝. Position the strips every ¾˝ down the length of the body, and attach them with a straight stitch. (Figure 2)

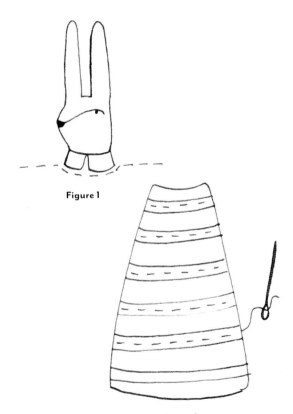

Figure 1

Figure 2

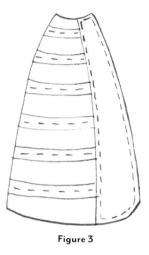

Figure 3

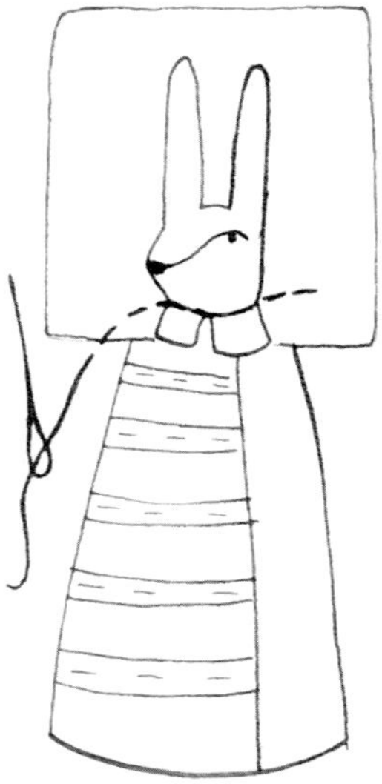

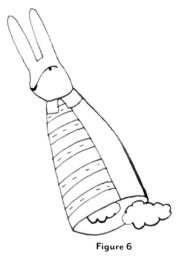

Figure 4

Figure 5

Figure 6

5. Cut out the jacket from the brown felt, and place it over the right side of the body. Stitch it in place. (Figure 3)

6. Align the head on top of the body, allowing enough overlap to stitch through both the head and the body. Sew along the neckline to secure it in place. (Figure 4)

7. Place Mr. Bunny on the cotton fabric, right sides together, making sure to extend the cotton ½" beyond the bottom of the felt piece. Sew Mr. Bunny to the cotton, ⅛" outside the edge of the embroidered design and with a ¼" seam allowance on the body. Leave the bottom section open. Trim any extra fabric from the sides and top, and clip the curved seams (page 9). (Figure 5)

8. Turn Mr. Bunny right side out, and fold the bottom cotton edge into the body. Stuff. (Figure 6)

9. Stand Mr. Bunny on top of the scrap of felt for the base, and trace around the base (see Figure 6, page 17). Cut out the felt, and attach it with a blanket stitch in light green embroidery floss.

ms. fox

FINISHED SIZE: 4½˝W × 5½˝H × 1¾˝D

An original wallhanging is always lovely to look at, especially when you are slyly gazed upon by Ms. Fox.

This project requires some skill, so you may want to give it a try after completing some less involved pieces first. After you have mastered this project, try out different frame shapes. Take those frames you have picked up at your local flea market, and translate them into felt. Wouldn't Ms. Fox look just that much more sly in a curvy, Victorian frame?

Materials

White wool felt: 4˝ × 5˝

Rust orange wool felt: 4˝ × 4˝

Bright orange wool felt: 2½˝ × 2½˝

Yellow ochre wool felt:
2 pieces each 5˝ × 6½˝

Patterned cotton fabric
for the back: 5˝ × 6½˝

Charcoal gray, orange, light
green, and light yellow
embroidery floss

Paper-backed fusible web: 9˝ × 9˝

Stuffing (page 7)

*The author used Holland Wool felt
in Soft White, Spice, Tangerine, and
Ochre (see Resources, page 94).*

Stitches

Straight stitch (page 11)

Back stitch (page 11)

Blanket stitch (page 12)

Cross stitch (page 12)

Satin stitch (page 13)

Whip stitch (page 13)

Instructions

Patterns are on page 78.

Background and Frame

1. Cut a 3¾˝ × 5˝ rectangle from the cotton fabric.

2. Cut a piece of fusible web the same size as the rectangle from Step 1. Follow the manufacturer's instructions to adhere it to the wrong side of the fabric.

3. Peel off the paper backing, and position the fabric in the center of the yellow ochre felt. Press with an iron to fuse the cotton to the felt.

4. Cut a 3˝ × 3˝ piece of white felt, and transfer Ms. Fox's dress using your preferred transfer method (pages 8–9). Then embroider the design. (Figure 1)

5. Cut a 3˝ × 3˝ piece of fusible web. Follow the manufacturer's instructions to adhere it to the wrong side of the dress. Cut out the dress shape along the dashed lines. Peel off the backing, and position the dress on the fabric, as shown. Fuse it in place, and set the piece aside. (Figure 2)

6. Cut out the frame from the yellow ochre felt, and pin it in place over Ms. Fox's dress and background. (The frame just needs to overlap the bottom of the dress a bit.) Make sure the bottom edge of the frame is level with the bottom edge of the back felt piece.

7. Starting at the inner edge of the frame, sew around the perimeter. Keep moving outward in one continuous motion until you have filled in the frame. Don't worry about making the lines perfectly parallel. In fact, try to allow for some natural line variation to make it more unique. (Figure 3)

8. Trim away any extra fabric that extends beyond the frame. (Figure 4)

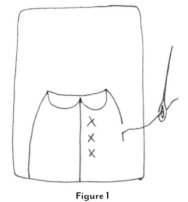

Figure 1

Figure 2

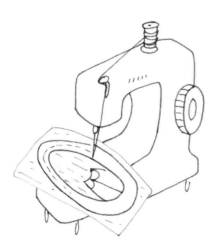

Figure 3

Figure 4

Ms. Fox's Head

1. Cut out the face pieces from the rust orange and white felt. Position the orange felt on top of the white felt, using the pattern as a guide. Embroider the design, making sure to go through both layers of felt. (Figure 5)

2. Cut out the ears from the bright orange felt. Pin the ears in position. (Figure 6)

3. Place the face on the remaining cotton fabric, right sides together. Sew around the outside of the face, ⅛" from the design, catching the ears in the seam. Leave one side open. Trim any extra fabric from the sides and top, and clip the curved seams (page 9). Turn the face right side out through the opening. Stuff. (Figure 7)

4. Sew the opening shut with a whip stitch in light green floss.

5. Embroider the fur marks on the face, referring to the pattern for guidance as needed. (Figure 8)

6. Using the pattern as a guide, position the head in place on the background and dress. Take this opportunity to try different angles for her head. With just a slight adjustment, you can completely change the feel of the piece and make her your own. Once you are happy with the look, come from the back of the fabric and use a few stitches to secure the head to the frame.

Final Assembly

1. For a more finished look, sew a blanket stitch around the perimeter of the frame in light yellow embroidery floss. Make sure to go through both layers of felt.

2. Attach a loop of floss onto the back. Congratulations—now you are ready to hang your very own Ms. Fox!

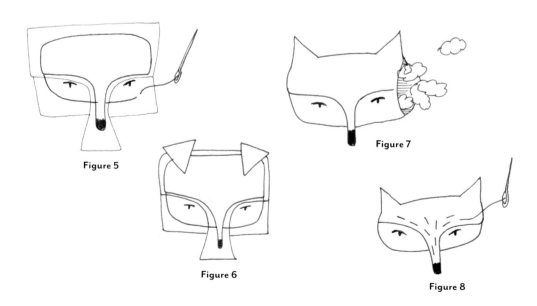

Figure 5

Figure 6

Figure 7

Figure 8

milly

FINISHED SIZE: 5¼˝W × 14˝H × 5˝D

After a long night of baking, Milly has put on her best apron and is ready to present the cake to the queen. (Let's hope the queen likes it!)

This project is a bit different from all the others, as it brings into play the added embellishment of the button. Not only does the button add a lovely aesthetic to the piece, it also adds functionality. With freedom to move the arms about, you can instantly change Milly's confident demeanor to a panicked one after dropping the cake right into the queen's lap. (Oh, dear!)

Materials

White wool felt:
1 piece 5½″ × 7″ for the head,
1 piece 3″ × 3½″ for the hands,
1 piece 3½″ × 4″ for the cake

Yellow ochre wool felt:
1 piece 7″ × 9″ for the dress,
2 pieces 2″ × 6½″ for the sleeves

Peach wool felt: ¼″ × 14″

Yellow wool felt: 4″ × 2″

Scraps of wool felt:
1 piece 6″ × 6″ for Milly's base,
1 piece 3″ × 4½″ for the cake's base

Patterned cotton:
2 pieces each 6½″ × 5″ for the apron,
1 piece 6″ × 15″ for the back,
2 pieces each 2″ × 10″ for the arms,
1 piece 3″ × 4″ for the cake back

Charcoal gray, light blue, turquoise,
and yellow embroidery floss

2 small buttons

Stuffing (page 7)

*The author used Holland Wool felt in
Soft White, Ochre, Flesh, and Yellow
(see Resources, page 94).*

Stitches

Straight stitch (page 11)

Back stitch (page 11)

Blanket stitch (page 12)

French knot (page 13)

Whip stitch (page 13)

Instructions

Patterns are on pages 79–80.

1. Use your preferred method (pages 8–9) to transfer Milly's face to the white felt. Embroider the design. Do not cut it out. (Figure 1)

2. Cut out the dress from the yellow ochre felt. Embroider the design. Position the dress in place over Milly's neck, and attach it by stitching across the top of the dress. (Figure 2)

3. Transfer the dress collar to the yellow felt. Embroider the design, and cut along the dashed lines (Figure 3). Pin the collar in position, and stitch it to the body along the top neckline of the collar using dark gray thread. (Make sure to position the collar slightly above the top line of the ochre dress.)

Figure 1

Figure 3

Figure 2

4. Place the 2 cotton apron pieces right sides together, place the apron pattern on the fabric, and cut out the 2 apron pieces. Sew the pieces together with a ¼˝ seam allowance. Leave the top edge open. Trim away the extra fabric, and clip or notch the curved seams (page 9). (Figure 4)

5. Turn the apron right side out, and press it flat with a hot iron. Turn the top edge ½˝ under, and press. Starting at the top right and using turquoise embroidery floss, whipstitch around the perimeter of the apron until you reach the top left corner. Pin the peach felt belt in position on the apron's top edge. Make sure to position the belt slightly higher than the folded top edge of the apron. Attach the belt to the apron with a straight stitch in light blue floss. Set aside.

6. Place Milly on the cotton back fabric, right sides together, making sure to extend the cotton ½˝ beyond the bottom of the felt piece. Sew Milly to the cotton, ⅛˝ outside the edge of the embroidered design and with a ¼˝ seam allowance along the dress. Leave the bottom section open. Trim any extra fabric from the sides and top, and clip the curved seams (page 9). (Figure 5)

7. Turn Milly right side out, and fold the bottom cotton edge into the body. Stuff. (Figure 6)

8. Stand Milly on top of a piece of felt, and trace around the base (see Figure 6, page 17). Cut out the felt, and attach it with a blanket stitch in yellow embroidery floss.

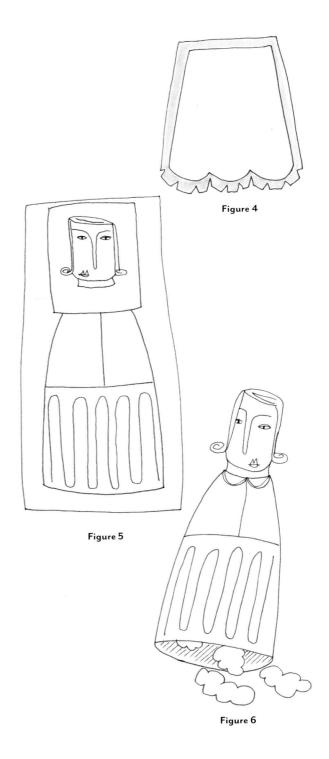

Figure 4

Figure 5

Figure 6

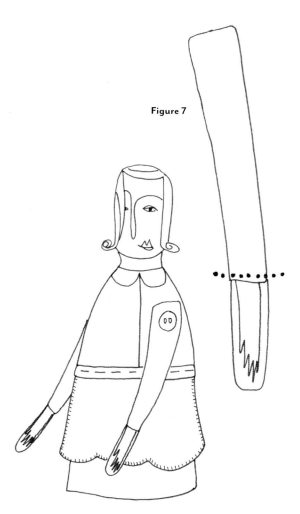

Figure 7

Figure 8

9. Transfer the hands to the white felt; embroider. Cut along the dashed lines. Cut out the first sleeve from the yellow ochre felt, and position it in place over one hand. Stitch along the edge of the sleeve. Place the arm on the cotton fabric, right sides together; sew them together, ⅛″ outside the edge of the hand design and with a ¼″ seam allowance on the sleeve. Leave the top of the sleeve open. Trim away the excess fabric, and clip any tight corners. Turn the arm inside out through the opening; stuff. Fold in the ends before closing the arm with a whip stitch in light blue floss. Repeat this step for the second arm. (Figure 7)

10. Position the arms, and pin them in place. Sew through the front arm and button. Then take the thread all the way through Milly's body, and sew through the back button and arm. Pull the thread firmly but not so tight that it indents the arm against the body. Repeat a few more times, and then knot the thread. This method will allow you to move the arms to any position you like. (Figure 8)

11. Transfer the cake to the white felt; embroider. Cut out the pattern, and place it on the 3″ × 4″ scrap of cotton fabric, right sides together, making sure to extend the cotton ½″ beyond the bottom of the felt piece. Sew the pieces together, and trim away any excess fabric. Leave the bottom open. Turn the cake right side out and fold the cotton bottom edge into the cake; stuff.

12. Trace the bottom of the cake onto the scrap of felt for the base (see Figure 6, page 17), and cut it out. Attach the felt piece to the bottom using a blanket stitch in light pink floss.

13. Tie on Milly's apron with a simple knot in the back.

my little village

FINISHED SIZE: EACH PIECE MEASURES APPROXIMATELY 3˝W × 3˝H × 2˝D

Lovely embroidered hills add a lot of delicious charm to this little village. Regardless of your skill level, this project is perfect for experimenting with decorative stitching and for making some of your own patterns. Fill one hill with an abundance of French knots in various colors; embroider another hill with rows and rows of split stitches. Have fun, and don't hold back.

Materials

White wool felt: 6˝ × 6˝

Orange wool felt: 6˝ × 4˝

Burnt orange wool felt: 5˝ × 4˝

Light green wool felt: 6˝ × 4˝

Green wool felt: 5˝ × 4˝

Blue wool felt: 2˝ × 3˝

Scraps of wool felt in colors of your choice for the bases of the hills: 2 pieces each 6˝ × 3½˝

Patterned cotton for the backs: 2 pieces each 6˝ × 4˝ for the hills, 1 piece 6˝ × 7˝ for the cottage

Charcoal gray, peach, light blue, turquoise, lime green, and orange embroidery floss

Stuffing (page 7)

The author used Holland Wool felt in Soft White, Tangerine, Spice, Willow, and Celery (see Resources, page 94).

Stitches

Straight stitch (page 11)

Seed stitch (page 11)

Back stitch (page 11)

Blanket stitch (page 12)

Whip stitch (page 13)

Instructions

Patterns are on pages 81–82.

Cottage

1. Use your preferred method (pages 8–9) to transfer the cottage design to the white felt. Embroider the design. Cut along the dashed lines. (Figure 1)

2. Transfer the roof design to the orange felt, and embroider the design lines in peach. Cut along the dashed lines. (Figure 2)

3. Position the roof on the embroidered white house, and pin it in place. Use charcoal colored thread to stitch along the designated baseline of the roof. Make sure to go through both layers of felt.

4. Cut out the door from the blue felt, and pin it in place. Use light blue embroidery floss to stitch around the edges in small straight stitches. Make sure to go through both layers of felt.

5. Place the cottage on the cotton fabric, right sides together. Sew the cottage to the fabric, ⅛˝ outside the edge of the design. Leave a 2˝ opening at the side. Trim away any excess fabric and felt, and notch any tight curves.

6. Turn the cottage right side out, and fold the cotton into the cottage. Stuff.

7. Close the opening with a whip stitch in matching thread.

Seeded Hill

1. Cut out the seeded hill from the burnt orange felt. Use the seeding technique (page 11) to embroider the hill in lime green embroidery floss. (Figure 3)

2. Place the hill on the cotton fabric, right sides together, making sure to extend the cotton ½˝ beyond the felt piece. Sew the hill to the fabric, using a ¼˝ seam allowance and leaving the bottom open. (Figure 4)

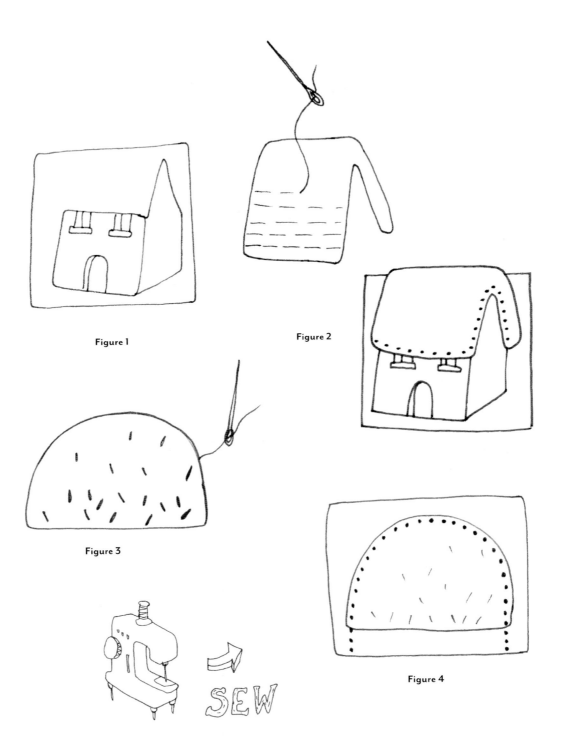

Figure 1

Figure 2

Figure 3

Figure 4

SEW

3. Trim the extra fabric from the sides and top. Turn the hill right side out, and fold the bottom cotton edge into the hill. Stuff.

4. Stand the hill on top of the piece of scrap felt for the base, and trace around the base (see Figure 6, page 17). Cut out the felt, and attach it with a blanket stitch in orange embroidery floss.

Striped Hill

1. Cut out the striped hill background from the light green felt. Cut out the hill stripes from the dark green felt. Using the pattern as a guide, pin the stripes in place on the hill. Use a straight stitch to embroider the stripes. Do not trim away any overhanging green felt yet. (Figure 5)

2. Place the hill on the cotton fabric, right sides together, making sure to extend the cotton ½˝ beyond the felt piece. Sew the hill to the fabric, using a ¼˝ seam allowance and leaving the bottom open. (Figure 6)

3. Trim away the extra fabric from the sides and top, and tuck the extra felt and bottom cotton edge into the hill. Turn the hill right side out, and fold the fabric into the hill. Stuff. (Figure 7)

4. Stand the hill on top of the piece of scrap felt, and trace around the base (see Figure 6, page 17). Cut out the felt, and attach it with a blanket stitch in light green embroidery floss.

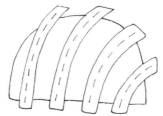

Figure 5

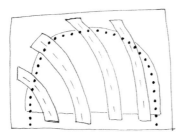

Figure 6

Figure 7

country cottage

FINISHED SIZE: 5½˝W × 7˝H × 3˝D

This cottage is a perfect place to visit for a nice cup of tea after a good long stroll through the countryside. This is a fast and easy project, so try whipping out some more cottages with different combinations of windows, doors, and shutters (pages 92–93). You'll have yourself a lovely little village in no time!

Materials

White wool felt:
1 piece 3˝ × 3˝ for the chimney,
1 piece 4½˝ × 7˝ for the facade

Yellow wool felt:
1 piece 7˝ × 5˝ for the roof,
1 piece 6˝ × 1½˝ for the top roofline

Yellow ochre wool felt: 3˝ × 3˝

Turquoise wool felt: 2˝ × 3˝

Scrap of wool felt in a color of
your choice for the base: 7˝ × 4˝

Patterned cotton
for the back: 7˝ × 8˝

Charcoal gray, cream, and
light blue embroidery floss

Stuffing (page 7)

*The author used Holland Wool felt in
Yellow, Soft White, Yellow Ochre, and
Turquoise (see Resources, page 94).*

Stitches

Straight stitch (page 11)

Back stitch (page 11)

Blanket stitch (page 12)

Instructions

Patterns are on pages 83–84.

1. Use your preferred method (pages 8–9) to transfer the house facade onto the white felt. Embroider the design, and cut along the dashed lines. (Figure 1)

2. Transfer the roof to the yellow felt. Embroider all the lines except for the bottom roofline; you will stitch that later when you attach the roof to the facade. Cut along the dashed lines.

3. Cut out the shutters from the yellow ochre felt, and pin them in place. Embroider with straight stitches, making sure to go through both layers of felt.

4. Transfer the door to the turquoise felt. Embroider the design. Cut along the dashed lines, and pin the door in place on the cottage. Using a matching sewing thread (or one-ply embroidery floss), stitch around the edge of the door through both layers of felt using a small, straight stitch. (Figure 2)

5. Using the pattern as a guide, place the roof in position, and pin to secure. To attach the roof to the cottage facade, stitch along the bottom of the roof in charcoal gray thread or floss. Make sure to go through both layers of felt.

6. Attach the top roofline at the top of the roof, making sure to overlap the edges a bit. Stitch along the bottom of the top roofline to attach it in place. (Figure 3)

7. Transfer the chimney to the white felt, and embroider the design. Place the chimney on the cotton, right sides together, and sew them together, ⅛˝ outside the edge of the design. Leave the bottom section open. Trim away any extra fabric, and clip or notch any tight curves (page 9). Turn the chimney right side out through the opening, and lightly stuff. Position the chimney upside down and cotton fabric side out when pinning it in place on the cottage roof. (Figure 4)

8. Place the cottage on the cotton fabric, right sides together, making sure to extend the cotton ½˝ beyond the bottom of the felt piece. Sew the cottage to the fabric, ⅛˝ outside the edge of the design. Leave the bottom section open. Trim the extra fabric from the sides and top, and notch any tight curves.

9. Turn the cottage right side out, and fold the bottom cotton edge into the cottage. Stuff.

10. Stand the cottage on top of the piece of scrap felt for the base, and trace around the base. (Figure 5)

11. Cut out the felt, and attach it using a blanket stitch with cream embroidery floss. (Figure 6)

Figure 1

Figure 2

Figure 3

Figure 4

Figure 5

Figure 6

across the pond

telephone booth

FINISHED SIZE: 3˝W × 7˝H × 2½˝D

This project is really fun to make, especially if you love the iconic, red telephone booths (or telephone boxes, if you want to be precise) as much as I do. Try turning the piece into an adorable ornament simply by attaching a loop of embroidery floss to the top.

Materials

Red wool felt: 5˝ × 8˝

White wool felt: 4˝ × 6½˝

Scrap of wool felt
for the base: 4˝ × 3˝

Patterned cotton
for the back: 4˝ × 8˝

Charcoal gray, pink, and
light blue embroidery floss

Stuffing (page 7)

*The author used Holland Wool
felt in Red and Soft White
(see Resources, page 94).*

Stitches

Straight stitch (page 11)

Back stitch (page 11)

Blanket stitch (page 12)

Whip stitch (page 13)

Instructions

Patterns are on pages 85.

1. Use your preferred method to transfer the telephone booth onto the red felt. Embroider the design (Figure 1). Following the pattern, cut out both window openings along the dashed lines. (Figure 2)

2. Use light blue embroidery floss to trace around the outside of each top panel with a straight stitch. (Figure 3)

3. Transfer the window onto the white felt. Stitch along the lines with charcoal thread. Cut out the window along the dashed lines, and pin in place behind the red telephone booth frame. Use a matching sewing thread (or one-ply embroidery floss) to whipstitch around the interior edge of both windows, making sure to go through both layers of felt.

4. Cut out the embroidered telephone booth along the dashed lines. Place the telephone booth on the cotton fabric, right sides together, making sure to extend the cotton at least ½˝ beyond the bottom of the felt piece. Sew the booth to the cotton, ⅛˝ outside the edge of the design. Leave the bottom section open. Trim any extra fabric from the sides and top, and clip any curved seams (page 9).

5. Turn the piece right side out through the opening. Fold the bottom cotton edge into the telephone booth. Stuff.

6. Stand the telephone booth on top of the piece of scrap felt, and trace around the base (see Figure 6, page 17). Cut out the felt, and attach it with a blanket stitch in pink embroidery floss.

Figure 1

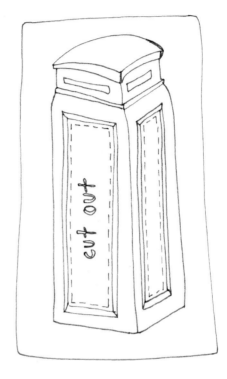

Figure 2

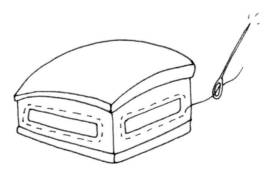

Figure 3

murray and the double-decker bus

FINISHED SIZES: 8˝W × 6˝H × 3˝D (BUS), 2˝W × 5˝H × 1½˝D (MURRAY)

Every Saturday, Murray takes a ride atop a magnificent cherry red bus. It's not just the views from the top that he finds so intriguing; it's the experience itself that makes it so magical. The passengers who ride the bus and the ads that adorn it make every bus unique. Customize your own double-decker bus by switching out the window and side panel patterns (page 88). Who will be riding on your bus today?

Materials

Double-Decker Bus

Red wool felt: 10˝ × 8˝

Bright red wool felt: 3˝ × 3½˝

White wool felt: 2 pieces each 8˝ × 2˝ for the top and bottom windows, 1 piece 1˝ × 2˝ for the wheels

Ochre wool felt: 5˝ × 8˝

Yellow wool felt: 9˝ × 2˝

Light gray wool felt: 3˝ × 2˝

Dark brown wool felt: 4˝ × 2˝

Patterned cotton for the back: 10˝ × 8˝

Charcoal gray and red embroidery floss

Stuffing (page 7)

The author used Holland Wool felt in Red, Salmon, Soft White, Marigold, Ochre, Cocoa, and Coffee (see Resources, page 94).

Stitches

Back stitch (page 11)

Whip stitch (page 13)

Blanket stitch (page 12)

Murray

White wool felt: 3˝ × 5˝

Ochre wool felt: 3½˝ × 3½˝

Scrap of wool felt for the base: 2½˝ × 2½˝

Patterned cotton for the back: 3½˝ × 5˝

Charcoal gray and yellow embroidery floss

Stuffing (page 7)

The author used Holland Wool felt in Soft White and Ochre (see Resources, page 94).

Instructions

Patterns are on pages 86–89.

Double-Decker Bus

1. Use your preferred method (pages 8–9) to transfer the bus onto the red felt. Embroider around the windows. Using the pattern as a guide, cut along the dashed lines within the windows and around the exterior of the design. (**Note:** If you are comfortable with free-motion stitching, embroider only the outline of the bus for this step.) (Figure 1)

Figure 1

2. Transfer the window strips (the outer solid window lines drawn on the bus pattern) onto the white felt, and cut them out. Position the window strips behind the open windows, and pin to secure. Use a matching sewing thread (or one-ply embroidery floss) to whipstitch around the interior edge of the windows, making sure to go through both layers of felt. (If you are free-motion stitching, simply sew over the window outlines with charcoal thread, making sure to go through both layers of felt.)

3. Transfer the main side panel (as drawn on the bus pattern) onto ochre felt, and cut it out. Transfer and cut out the "biscuit" letters from the yellow felt, and position them on the ochre panel. Follow along the letters with a backstitch in charcoal thread. (Use this opportunity to be more free with your sewing. Try not to worry about it looking too perfect. This is also a great opportunity for free-motion stitching.) (Figure 2) Pin the embroidered main panel in place on the bus. Embroider around the inside edge of the panel with charcoal gray floss, making sure to go through both layers of felt. (Figure 3)

4. Transfer the small side panel and the front sign (as drawn on the bus pattern) onto light gray felt, and cut out each piece. Embroider the number "6" on the small side panel, and position it in place on the bus. Embroider around the inside edge of the panel in charcoal gray embroidery floss, making sure to go through both layers of felt. Repeat to attach the front sign in place. (Figure 3)

5. Transfer the back door onto ochre felt, and cut it out. Embroider the design and pin it in place. Using matching thread for each piece, whipstitch around the exposed edges, making sure to go through both layers of felt. (Figure 3)

6. Transfer the long side strip (as drawn on the bus pattern) onto the yellow felt, and cut it out. Pin it in place on the bus, making sure to overlap the top of the back door (Figure 4). Backstitch the strip in place in charcoal gray floss, making sure to go through both layers of felt.

7. Transfer the front hood piece onto the bright red felt, and cut it out. Embroider the design, and pin it in place on the bus. Transfer the front grate onto the ochre felt, and cut it out. Embroider the design, and pin it in place on top of the hood. Using matching thread for each piece, whipstitch around the exposed edges, making sure to go through both layers of felt (Figure 4).

8. With right sides facing each other, pin the bus to the cotton fabric. Sew around the edges, ⅛" outside the edge of the design. Leave a 3" opening at the bottom. Trim the extra fabric, and clip or notch any tight curves. Turn the bus right side out through the opening. Stuff. (Figure 5)

9. Stitch the opening closed using a hidden stitch in a matching thread.

10. Cut out the wheels from the dark brown felt. Cut out 2 wheel hubs from scraps of white felt. Position a hub on each wheel. Using dark brown floss, come from behind the white felt to sew a series of intersecting lines to create the wheel design. (Figure 6)

11. Cut out 2 scraps of cotton fabric slightly larger than each wheel. With right sides together, sew around the edges, leaving the top of each wheel open. Trim off any excess fabric from the sides and bottom. Turn the wheels right side out and fold the cotton edge into the wheel. Stuff. (Figure 7)

Figure 2

Figure 3

Figure 4

Figure 5

Figure 7

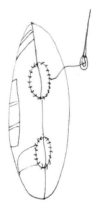

Figure 8

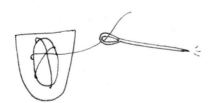

Figure 6

12. Pin the wheels in place on the bus, and attach using a whip stitch in brown floss around the entire top perimeter of each wheel. (Figure 8)

Murray

1. Use your preferred method (pages 8–9) to transfer Murray's face and torso onto the white felt. Embroider the design, but do not cut it out yet. (Figure 1)

2. Transfer the jacket design onto the ochre felt, and then embroider it. Cut out the jacket along the dashed lines. Attach the jacket to Murray's face and torso by stitching along the top edge of the jacket. (Figure 2)

3. Place Murray on the cotton fabric, right sides together, making sure to extend the cotton ½˝ beyond the bottom of the felt piece. Sew Murray to the cotton, ⅛˝ outside the edge of the design. Leave the bottom section open. Trim any extra fabric from the sides and top, and clip the curved seams (page 9).

4. Turn Murray right side out, and fold the bottom cotton edge into the body. Stuff. (Figure 3)

5. Stand the figure on top of the scrap of felt for the base, and trace around the base (see Figure 6, page 17). Cut out the felt, and attach it with a blanket stitch in yellow embroidery floss.

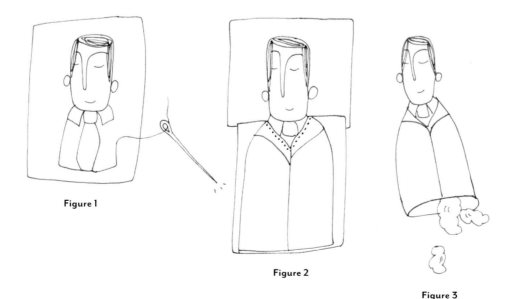

Figure 1

Figure 2

Figure 3

mr. milkman

FINISHED SIZE: 5˝W × 7˝H × 4˝D

Apron tied securely and hat freshly pressed, Mr. Milkman is ready to start his morning deliveries. The sound of his clanging glass milk bottles approaching everyone's door makes him a favorite in the neighborhood. Who doesn't love that?

This may be the most challenging project in the book, but the rewards will be ever so worth it in the end. Try adjusting the position of his legs. With freedom to bend the legs in any direction, you may give Mr. Milkman a moment to sit before heading back out for his afternoon deliveries.

Materials

White wool felt:
1 piece 7½˝ × 7˝ for the body,
1 piece 6˝ × 4½˝ for the wings,
1 piece 3˝ × 3˝ for the milk bottles

Yellow ochre wool felt: 9˝ × 5˝

Light brown wool felt:
1 piece 5˝ × 6˝ for the bag,
1 piece ¼˝ × 10¾˝ for the bag strap

Dark brown wool felt: 3½˝ × 6˝

Patterned cotton: 1 piece 7½˝ × 7˝
for the back of the bird,
1 piece 3˝ × 3˝ for the milk jugs,
1 piece 4˝ × 3˝ for the apron,
1 piece 1˝ × 12˝ for the apron belt

Light blue, cream, and dark
brown embroidery floss

Orange wool thread (*The author
used three-ply Persian wool.*)

Wire (16 gauge) for bird legs:
1 piece 11˝ long

Stuffing (page 7)

*The author used Holland Wool felt
in Soft White, Ochre, Coffee, and
Mocha (see Resources, page 94).*

Stitches

Straight stitch (page 11)

Back stitch (page 11)

Whip stitch (page 13)

Instructions

Patterns are on pages 90–91.

1. Use your preferred method (pages 8–9) to transfer Mr. Milkman's body to the white felt. Embroider the design, but do not cut it out yet. (Figure 1)

2. Transfer the jacket to the yellow ochre felt, and embroider the design. Cut out the jacket along the dashed lines, and pin it in place on Mr. Milkman's body, using the diagram as a guide. Attach the jacket by stitching along the collar's edge. (Figure 2)

3. For each wing, transfer the pattern to the white felt piece, and embroider the design. Cut out the first sleeve from the yellow ochre felt, and position it in place over one wing. Attach it by stitching along the bottom edge of the sleeve. (Figure 3)

4. Place the wing unit on the cotton fabric, right sides together, and sew them together, ⅛˝ outside the edge of the design and with a ¼˝ seam allowance on the sleeve. Leave one side of the sleeve open. Trim away any excess fabric, and clip any tight corners. Turn the wing inside out through the opening; stuff. Fold in the edges before closing with a whip stitch in light blue floss. Repeat this step for the second wing.

5. Place Mr. Milkman's body on the cotton fabric, right sides together. Sew around the outside of the bird, again ⅛˝ outside the edge of the design. Leave a 2˝ opening at the base (refer to the pattern for placement of the opening). Trim off the extra felt and fabric (do not cut any off the bottom of the jacket), and carefully cut little notches around any curved sections to allow for a smoother shape when finished. Turn Mr. Milkman right side out, and fold the cotton and felt into the body (except for the bottom of the jacket—let that hang out). Stuff most of the bird, but leave the area at the bottom free of stuffing; do not stitch closed yet.

6. To prepare the wire legs, bend the wire in half. Using a pair of pliers, bend in 1¼˝ at the bottom of each end to create the foot, forming an L-shape on each end. Take the end of each wire, and bend it inward, using the diagram as a guide. Starting on one end, wrap the entire leg with orange wool thread, making sure to cover any exposed wire. Secure the thread with a tight knot, and trim away any excess thread. (Figure 4) You can also use a large threaded needle and sew through the wrapped wool thread back and forth a couple of times to secure. Trim away any extra thread.

7. Position the wired legs on the body, and finish stuffing the bird, thus securing the legs inside the body. Using any scrap wool felt available, cut out a piece of wool slightly larger than the opening left at the base of the bird. Tuck the felt under the opening (again making sure to let the bottom of the jacket hang freely outside), and whipstitch it in place. (Figure 5) Stand Mr. Milkman, and bend the legs as necessary to allow a free-standing position.

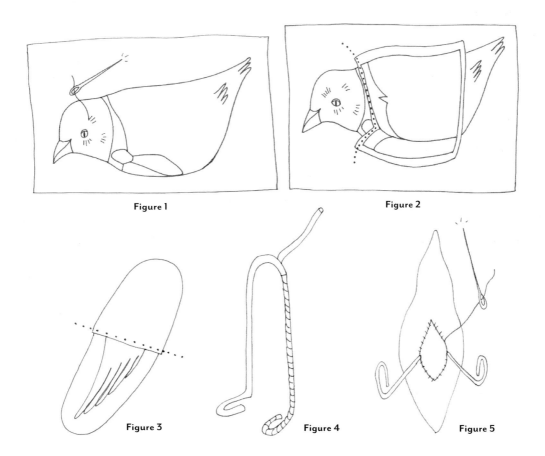

Figure 1

Figure 2

Figure 3

Figure 4

Figure 5

8. To finish the edges of the apron, fold under ¼˝ on each apron side; press. Fold again, and press once more. Do the same for the apron's bottom edge. Sew around all 3 sides of the apron, using a ⅛˝ seam allowance (Figure 6). Fold under ¼˝ along the belt's long edges; press. Center the belt over the top of the apron, and stitch it together (Figure 7). Use scissors to trim the loose belt ends on a diagonal. Tie the apron around Mr. Milkman's waist.

9. Pin the wings in the desired positions. (Have fun with this. By simply changing the direction and position of the wings, you can really personalize your bird.) Attach the top of each wing to Mr. Milkman's body with a whip stitch in the thread of your choice.

10. For Mr. Milkman's bag, start at the bottom center of the bag, and attach the strap to the bag's front and back using a simple straight stitch in yellow embroidery floss.

11. To make the hat, attach the hat band to the top of the hat with a straight stitch in light blue embroidery floss. When you have sewn all around the perimeter of the hat, simply tuck the extra band behind. (Figure 8)

12. Position the brim just under the widest part of the band, and attach it with more straight stitches along the bottom edge of the band. Continue the straight stitch around the entire base of the brim.

13. Transfer the milk jug pattern to white felt, and embroider the design. Place the milk jugs on the cotton fabric, right sides together, making sure to extend the bottom ½˝ beyond the bottom of the felt. Sew around the edges, leaving the bottom open. Trim off any extra fabric from the sides and top, and clip the curved seams (page 9). Turn the piece right side out, and fold the bottom cotton edge inside. Stuff. Trace the bottom of the milk jugs onto a scrap of felt for the base (see Figure 6, page 17), and cut it out. Attach the felt piece to the bottom with a blanket stitch in cream floss.

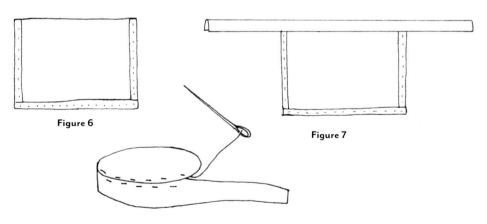

Figure 6

Figure 7

Figure 8

Smashing Scones ...

Ingredients

2 cups flour

1/3 cup sugar

2 tsp baking powder

1/2 tsp salt

1/2 cup chopped butter

2 eggs

1 tsp vanilla

1/4 cup orange juice

orange peel (optional)

1/3 cup currants

Instructions

① mix together dry ingredients

② add chopped butter and mix until crumbs form

③ add raisins. mix

four. in separate bowl, mix together eggs, orange juice, and vanilla. (add peel for fun!)

⑤ quickly add wet to dry... stir just to combine

six. turn onto greased cookie sheet and pat into 1 1/2" thick circle

⑦ cut into triangles and glaze with milk.

⑧ bake at 425°f for ~ 25 min.

enjoy with ...

pot

cup

scone

butter

jam . . . .

patterns

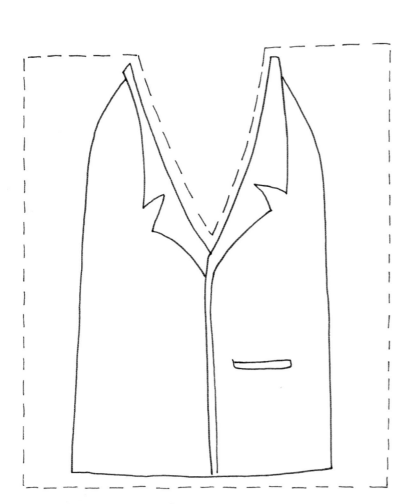

Charles
Charcoal gray back stitch

Charles's jacket
Light gray back stitch

Charles's mustache

Charles's vest
Dark blue back stitch

CHARLES OPTIONS

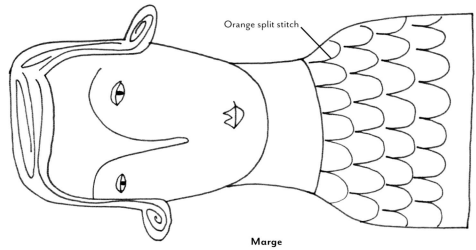

Orange split stitch

Marge
Charcoal gray back stitch

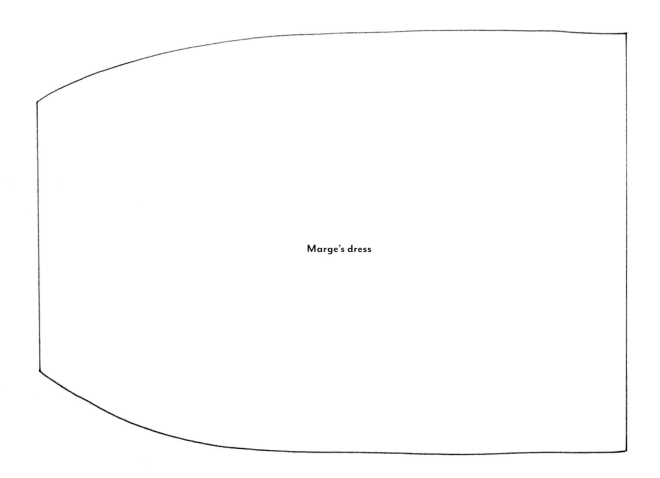

Marge's dress

Polly

mauve

tizzy

zeander

Alternate Marge faces

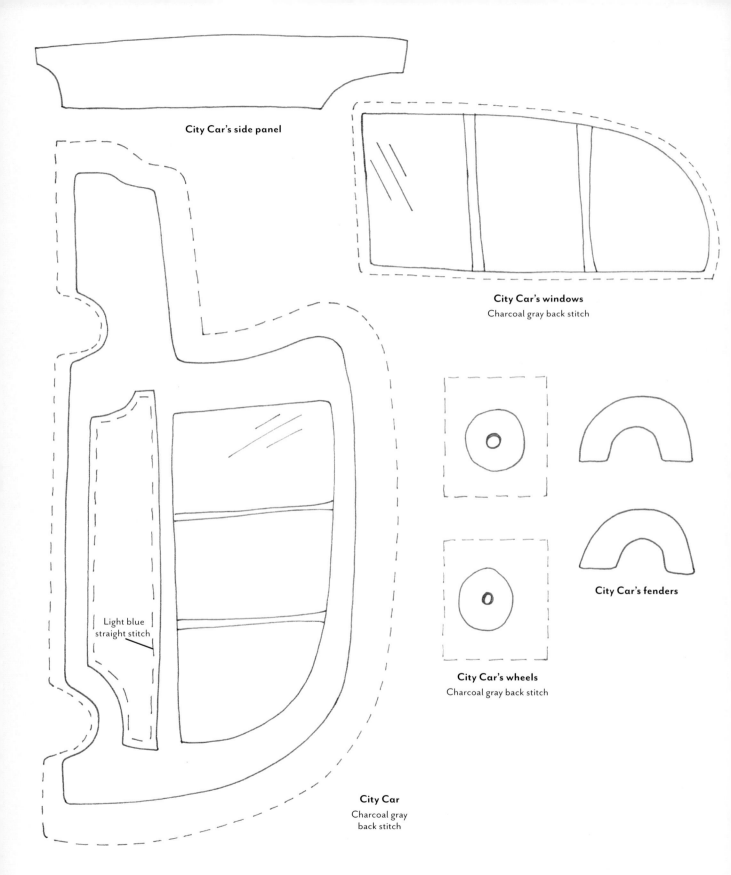

City Car's side panel

City Car's windows
Charcoal gray back stitch

Light blue
straight stitch

City Car's fenders

City Car's wheels
Charcoal gray back stitch

City Car
Charcoal gray
back stitch

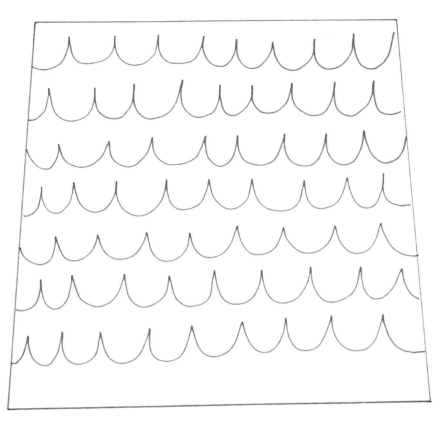

Brownstone roof

Charcoal gray back stitch (or split stitch)

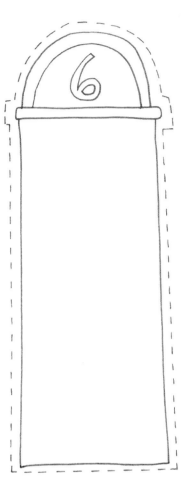

Brownstone door background

Charcoal gray back stitch

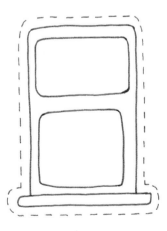

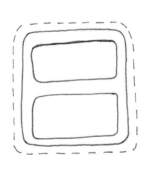

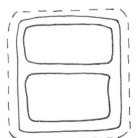

Brownstone windows

Charcoal gray back stitch for all windows

Brownstone chimney

Charcoal gray back stitch

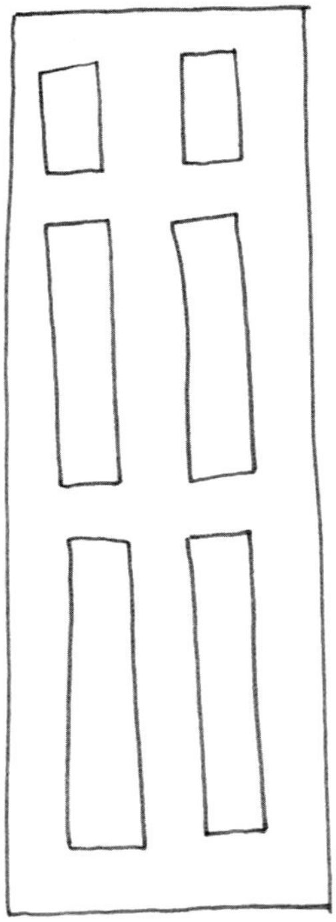

**Brownstone door
and panel shapes**

Cut out 7 pieces total.

Brownstone shutters

Cut 4.

**Brownstone window
adornments**

Cut 3.

Brownstone house shape

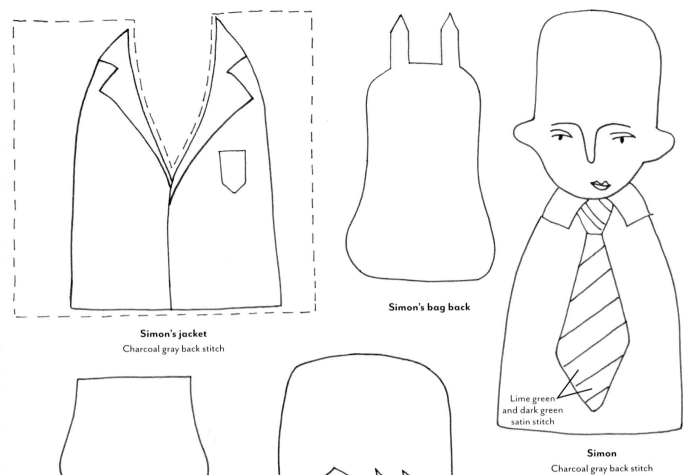

Simon's jacket
Charcoal gray back stitch

Simon's bag back

Simon
Charcoal gray back stitch

Lime green
and dark green
satin stitch

Simon's bag front

Simon's hair
Tan back stitch

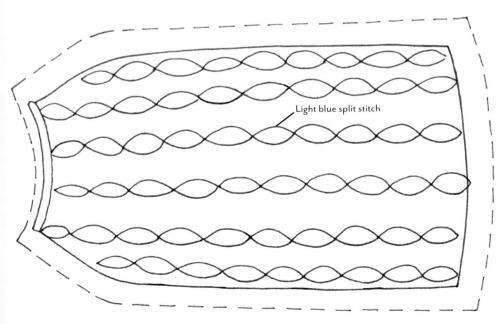

Light blue split stitch

Collin's sweater
Charcoal gray back stitch

patterns   75

Collin's mustache

Collin
Charcoal gray back stitch

Alternate sweaters for Collin

fanciful felties

Mr. Bunny
Charcoal gray back stitch and satin stitch

Mr. Bunny's mustache

Mr. Bunny's jacket
Charcoal gray back stitch

Mr. Bunny's body
Light green straight stitch

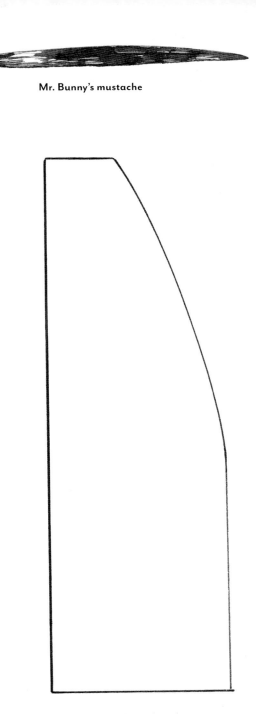

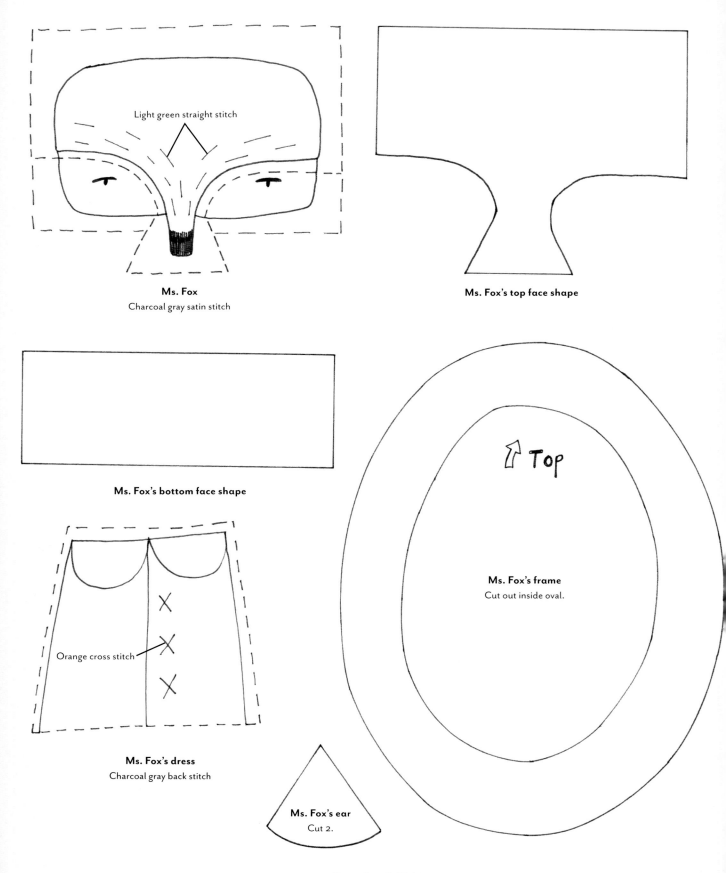

Ms. Fox
Charcoal gray satin stitch

Light green straight stitch

Ms. Fox's top face shape

Ms. Fox's bottom face shape

Ms. Fox's frame
Cut out inside oval.

↑ TOP

Orange cross stitch

Ms. Fox's dress
Charcoal gray back stitch

Ms. Fox's ear
Cut 2.

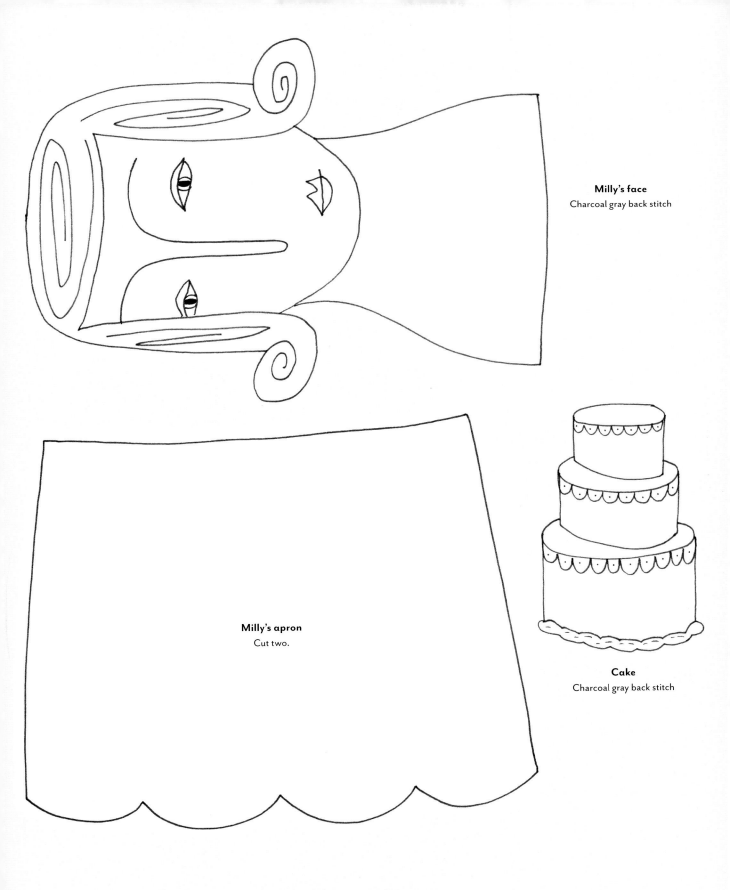

Milly's face
Charcoal gray back stitch

Milly's apron
Cut two.

Cake
Charcoal gray back stitch

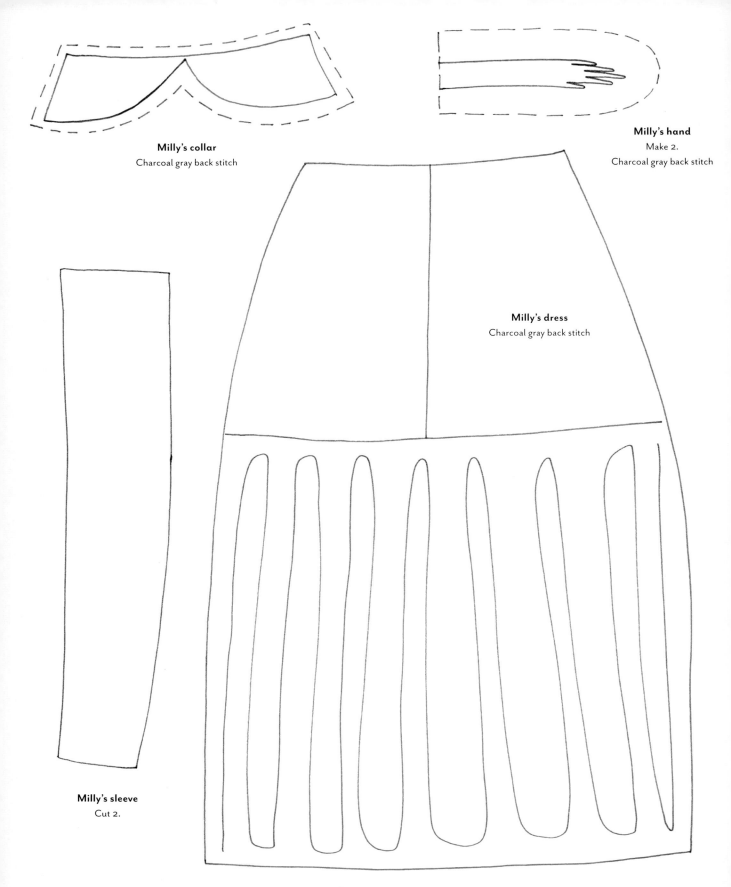

Milly's collar
Charcoal gray back stitch

Milly's hand
Make 2.
Charcoal gray back stitch

Milly's dress
Charcoal gray back stitch

Milly's sleeve
Cut 2.

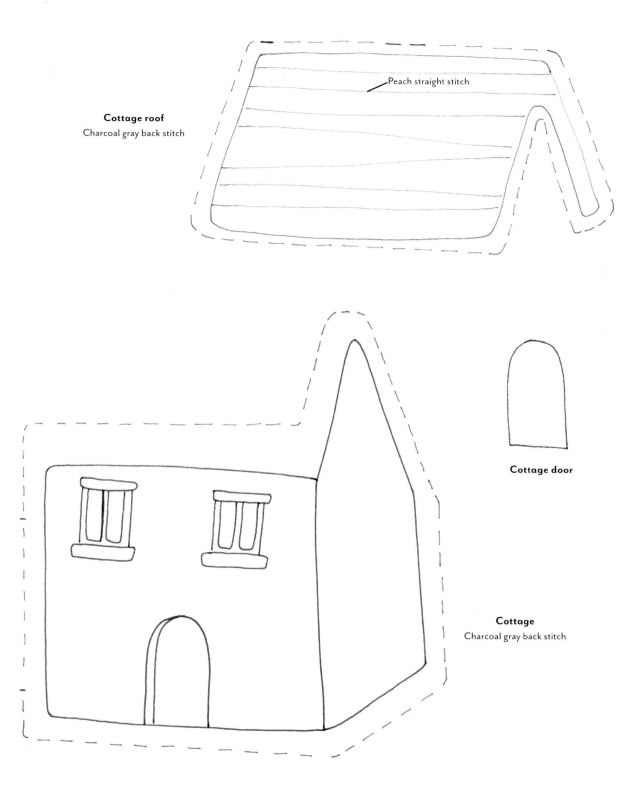

Cottage roof
Charcoal gray back stitch

Peach straight stitch

Cottage door

Cottage
Charcoal gray back stitch

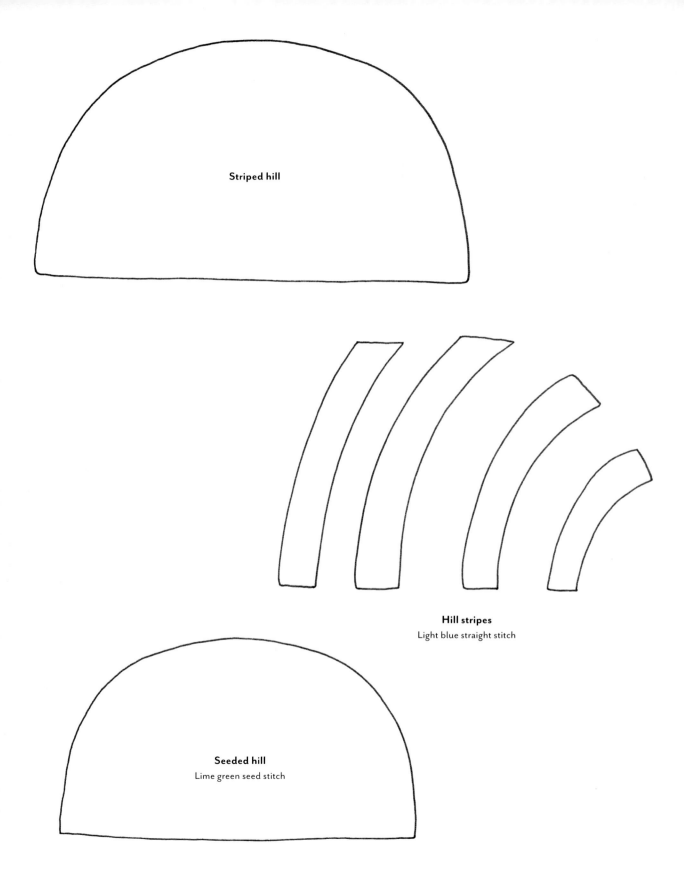

Striped hill

Hill stripes
Light blue straight stitch

Seeded hill
Lime green seed stitch

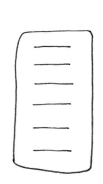

Country cottage shutter
Cut 2.
Light blue straight stitch

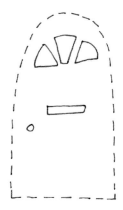

Country cottage door
Charcoal gray back stitch

Country cottage chimney
Charcoal gray back stitch

Country cottage
Charcoal gray back stitch

Country cottage thatched top roofline

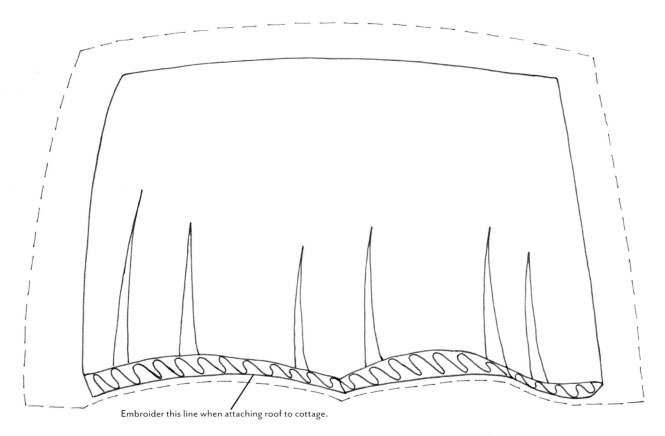

Embroider this line when attaching roof to cottage.

Country cottage roof
Charcoal gray back stitch

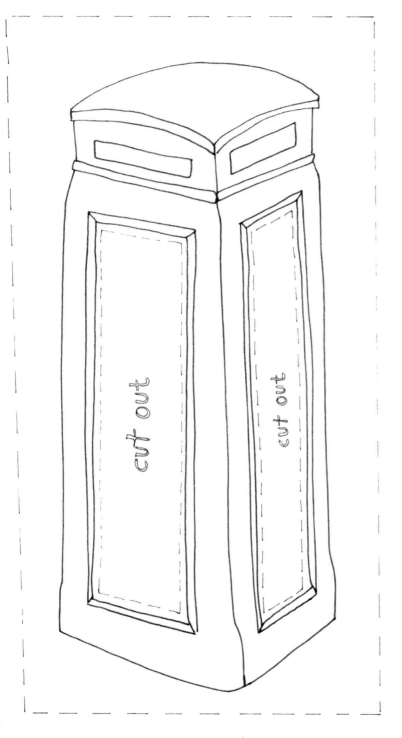

cut out

cut out

Telephone booth
Charcoal gray back stitch

Telephone booth windows
Charcoal gray back stitch

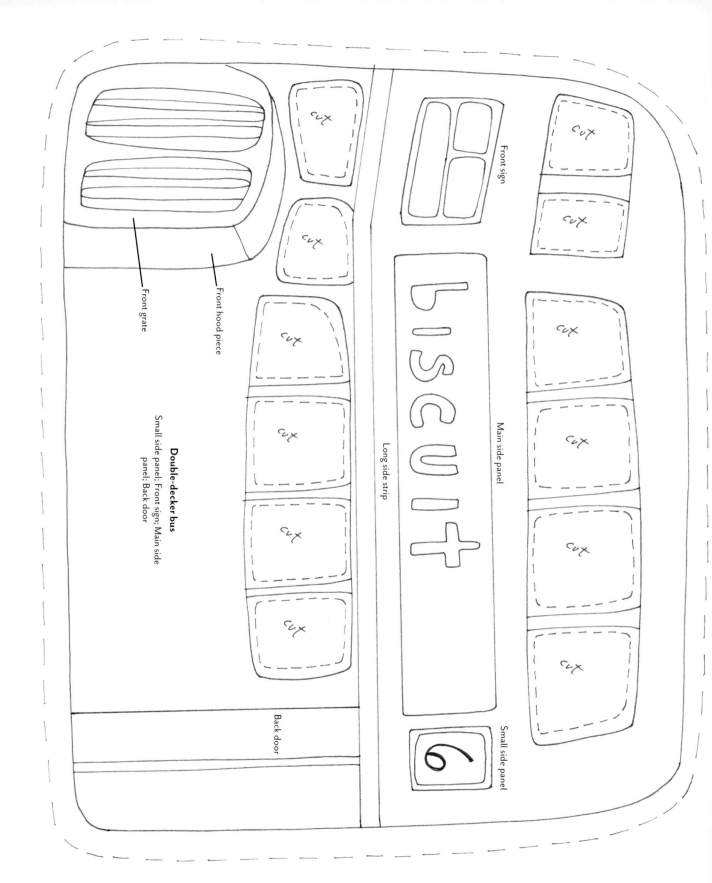

Front grate

Front hood piece

Double-decker bus
Small side panel; Front sign; Main side
panel; Back door

cut

cut

cut

cut

cut

cut

Back door

Long side strip

biscuit

6

Front sign

Main side panel

cut

cut

cut

cut

cut

cut

Small side panel

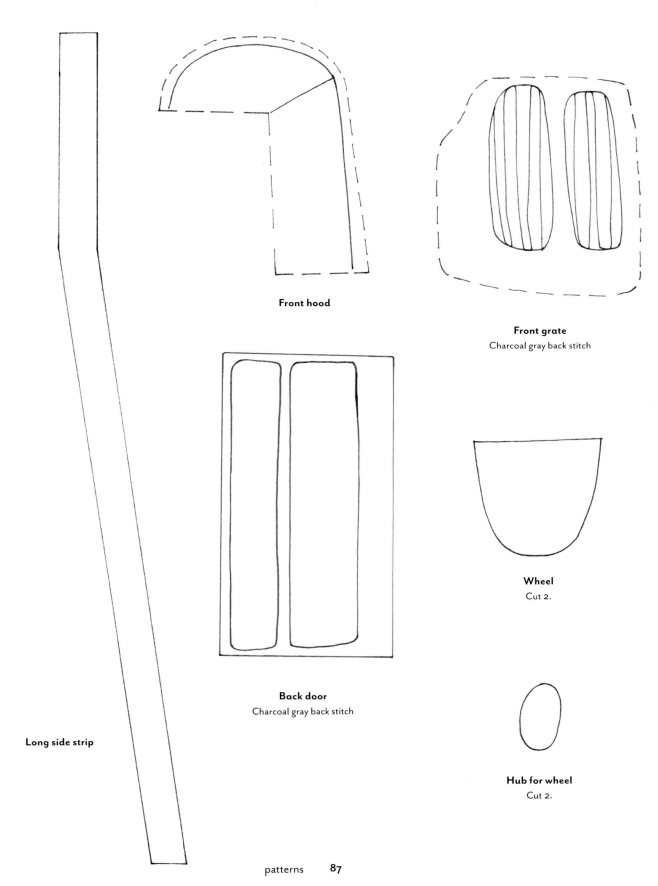

Front hood

Front grate
Charcoal gray back stitch

Wheel
Cut 2.

Back door
Charcoal gray back stitch

Long side strip

Hub for wheel
Cut 2.

bUnnY BISCUITS CO.

TILLY TEAS

BUS Transport CO.

Options for bus side panel

Options for bus windows

Murray's face and torso
Charcoal gray back stitch

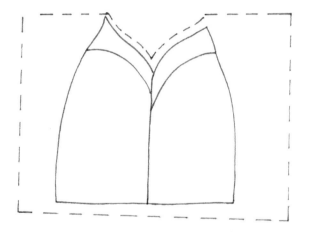

Murray's jacket
Charcoal gray back stitch

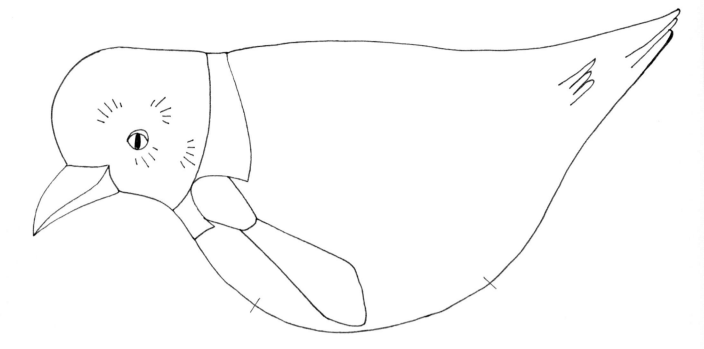

Mr. Milkman
Charcoal gray back stitch

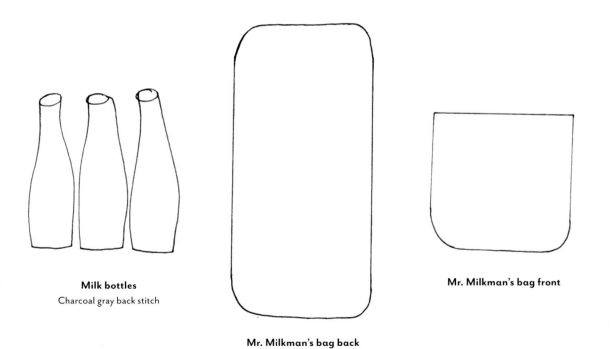

Milk bottles
Charcoal gray back stitch

Mr. Milkman's bag front

Mr. Milkman's bag back

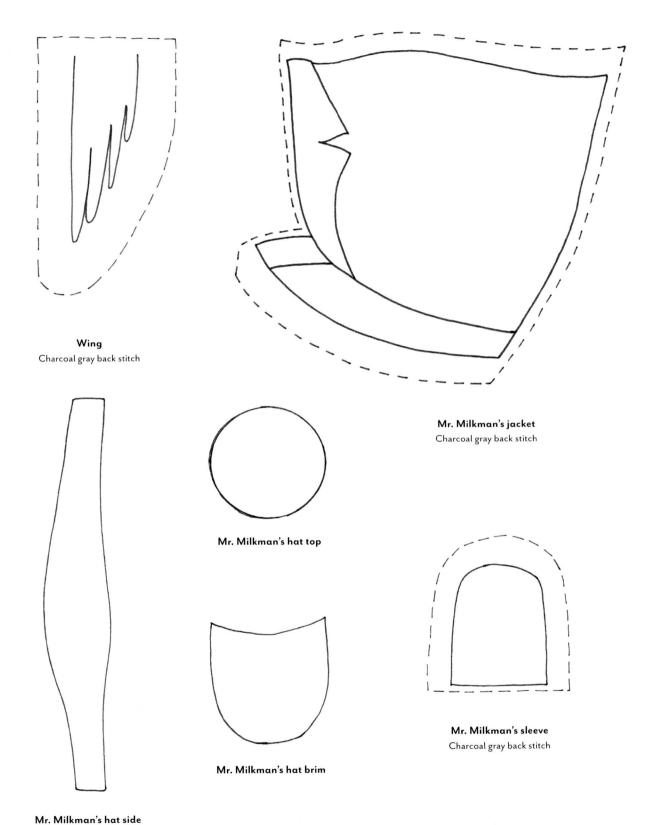

Wing
Charcoal gray back stitch

Mr. Milkman's jacket
Charcoal gray back stitch

Mr. Milkman's hat top

Mr. Milkman's sleeve
Charcoal gray back stitch

Mr. Milkman's hat brim

**Mr. Milkman's hat side
(band)**

Options for windows

resources

FELT

A Child's Dream Come True
www.achildsdream.com
800-359-2906

Here you'll find an amazing selection of pure wool felt. The colors alone will make you drool. If you are anything like me, you will be hooked once that first package arrives.

Magic Cabin
www.magiccabin.com
888-623-3655

Another source of high-quality, medium-weight felt. A popular site for many a crafter!

FABRIC

Robert Kaufman
www.robertkaufman.com
800-877-2066

I am so grateful for the opportunity to design a line of fabric for this fantastic company. Please visit the website for more information.

Hawthorne Threads
www.hawthornethreads.com

Known by many in the Etsy community as Fabric Supplies, this fantastic business is run by the husband-and-wife team of Charlie and Lindsay Prezzano. They specialize in contemporary cotton from a plethora of designers at a discounted price and are truly the most wonderful people to work with.

Reprodepot Fabric
www.reprodepotfabrics.com
help@reprodepot.com

I had the wonderful opportunity of seeing Reprodepot Fabric table at a show in New York City and was blown away by the selection. An affordable opportunity to choose from a unique selection of fabulous vintage reproduction, retro fabrics, Japanese import fabrics, and Marimekko textiles.

PurlSoho
www.purlsoho.com
800-597-7875

PurlSoho has an incredible collection of hand-picked fabrics that will surely inspire many a project.

RETAIL STORES

Michaels
www.michaels.com
800-642-4235

Somehow I always manage to leave this shop with much more than I had intended to buy. Thank goodness I go with two little kids in tow; otherwise, countless hours would be spent browsing through the endless selection of craft supplies.

Hancock Fabrics
www.hancockfabrics.com
877-322-7427

Do my thoughts about Michaels give you any indication of how I might feel about this one as well?

INSPIRATIONAL READING

Craft

www.craftzine.com

Save your copies of this magazine, and keep them easily accessible. They are quite handy when you need a little extra inspiration.

Selvedge

www.selvedge.org

This British magazine is one of my favorite materials to read. Their aesthetic is like none other and definitely worth the money.

Embroidery

http://embroidery.embroiderersguild.com

The first copy I managed to get my hands on started what I am sure will be a lifelong love for this publication. Absolutely beautiful.

For a list of other fine books from C&T Publishing, ask for a free catalog:

C&T Publishing, Inc.
P.O. Box 1456
Lafayette, CA 94549
800-284-1114

Email: ctinfo@ctpub.com
Website: www.ctpub.com

For sewing supplies:
Cotton Patch
1025 Brown Avenue
Lafayette, CA 94549
Store: 925-284-1177
Mail order: 925-283-7883

Email: CottonPa@aol.com
Website: www.quiltusa.com

Note: Fabrics used in the projects shown may not be currently available, as fabric manufacturers keep most fabrics in print for only a short time.

about the author

British-born Samantha Cotterill is a self-taught fiber artist who lives in upstate New York with her husband and two young boys. Samantha began her career as a professional painter before taking time off to focus on family. Five years later, she returned to the art world with the launching of mummysam, an online shop featuring her hand-sewn creations. In 2009, Samantha teamed up with Robert Kaufman to design a mummysam line of fabric that hit the market in summer 2010. She currently works out of her home studio, where she hopes to continue a lifelong journey of writing, designing, and creating. Visit her at mummysam.com.

Photo by Thea Coughlin

stashBOOKS

fabric arts for a handmade lifestyle

If you're craving beautiful authenticity in a time of mass-production...Stash Books is for you. Stash Books is a new line of how-to books celebrating fabric arts for a handmade lifestyle. Backed by C&T Publishing's solid reputation for quality, Stash Books will inspire you with contemporary designs, clear and simple instructions, and engaging photography.

www.stashbooks.com